MAX LUCADO

LIFE LESSONS *from*

PHILIPPIANS

Guide to Joy

PREPARED BY THE LIVINGSTONE CORPORATION

THOMAS NELSON
Since 1798

Published in Nashville, Tennessee, by Thomas Nelson. Thomas Nelson is a registered trademark of HarperCollins Christian Publishing, Inc.

Produced with the assistance of the Livingstone Corporation. Project staff include Jake Barton, Joel Bartlett, Andy Culbertson, Mary Horner Collins, Will Reaves, and Rachel Hawkins.

Editor: Len Woods

All Scripture quotations, unless otherwise indicated, are taken from The Holy Bible, New International Version®, NIV®. Copyright © 1973, 1978, 1984, 2011 by Biblica, Inc.™ Used by permission. All rights reserved worldwide.

Scripture quotations marked NCV are taken from the New Century Version®. Copyright © 2005 by Thomas Nelson. Used by permission. All rights reserved.

Scripture quotations marked NKJV are taken from the New King James Version®. Copyright © 1982 by Thomas Nelson. Used by permission. All rights reserved.

Scripture quotations marked NLT are taken from the Holy Bible, New Living Translation, copyright © 1996, 2004, 2015 by Tyndale House Foundation. Used by permission of Tyndale House Publishers, Inc., Carol Stream, Illinois 60188. All rights reserved

Material for the "Inspiration" sections taken from the following books:

The Applause of Heaven. Copyright © 1990 by Max Lucado. Thomas Nelson, a registered trademark of HarperCollins Christian Publishing, Inc., Nashville, Tennessee.

Anxious for Nothing. Copyright © 2017 by Max Lucado. Thomas Nelson, a registered trademark of HarperCollins Christian Publishing, Inc., Nashville, Tennessee.

Because of Bethlehem. Copyright © 2016 by Max Lucado. Thomas Nelson, a registered trademark of HarperCollins Christian Publishing, Inc., Nashville, Tennessee

Cure for the Common Life. Copyright © 2005 by Max Lucado. Thomas Nelson, a registered trademark of HarperCollins Christian Publishing, Inc., Nashville, Tennessee.

The Great House of God. Copyright © 1997 by Max Lucado. Thomas Nelson, a registered trademark of HarperCollins Christian Publishing, Inc., Nashville, Tennessee.

It's Not About Me. Copyright © 2004 by Max Lucado. Integrity Publishers, Brentwood, Tennessee.

Next Door Savior. Copyright © 2003 by Max Lucado. Thomas Nelson, a registered trademark of HarperCollins Christian Publishing, Inc., Nashville, Tennessee.

Shaped by God (previously published as *On the Anvil*). © 2001 by Max Lucado. Tyndale House Publishers, Carol Stream, Illinois 60188.

Six Hours One Friday. Copyright © 2004 by Max Lucado. Thomas Nelson, a registered trademark of HarperCollins Christian Publishing, Inc., Nashville, Tennessee.

Thomas Nelson titles may be purchased in bulk for educational, business, fundraising, or sales promotional use. For information, please e-mail SpecialMarkets@ThomasNelson.com.

ISBN 978-0-310-08650-5

First Printing May 2018 / Printed in the United States of America

CONTENTS

HOW TO STUDY THE BIBLE

The Bible is a peculiar book. Words crafted in another language. Deeds done in a distant era. Events recorded in a far-off land. Counsel offered to a foreign people. It is a peculiar book.

It's surprising that anyone reads it. It's too old. Some of its writings date back 5,000 years. It's too bizarre. The book speaks of incredible floods, fires, earthquakes, and people with supernatural abilities. It's too radical. The Bible calls for undying devotion to a carpenter who called himself God's Son.

Logic says this book shouldn't survive. Too old, too bizarre, too radical.

The Bible has been banned, burned, scoffed, and ridiculed. Scholars have mocked it as foolish. Kings have branded it as illegal. A thousand times over the grave has been dug and the dirge has begun, but somehow the Bible never stays in the grave. Not only has it survived, but it has also thrived. It is the single most popular book in all of history. It has been the bestselling book in the world for years!

There is no way on earth to explain it. Which perhaps is the only explanation. For the Bible's durability is not found on *earth* but in *heaven*. The millions who have tested its claims and claimed its promises know there is but one answer: the Bible is God's book and God's voice.

As you read it, you would be wise to give some thought to two questions: *What is the purpose of the Bible?* and *How do I study the Bible?* Time spent reflecting on these two issues will greatly enhance your Bible study.

What is the purpose of the Bible?

Let the Bible itself answer that question: *"From infancy you have known the Holy Scriptures, which are able to make you wise for salvation through faith in Christ Jesus"* (2 Timothy 3:15).

The purpose of the Bible? Salvation. God's highest passion is to get his children home. His book, the Bible, describes his plan of salvation. The purpose of the Bible is to proclaim God's plan and passion to save his children.

This is the reason why this book has endured through the centuries. It dares to tackle the toughest questions about life: *Where do I go after I die? Is there a God? What do I do with my fears?* The Bible is the treasure map that leads to God's highest treasure—eternal life.

But how do you study the Bible? Countless copies of Scripture sit unread on bookshelves and nightstands simply because people don't know how to read it. What can you do to make the Bible real in your life?

The clearest answer is found in the words of Jesus: *"Ask and it will be given to you; seek and you will find; knock and the door will be opened to you"* (Matthew 7:7).

The first step in understanding the Bible is asking God to help you. You should read it prayerfully. If anyone understands God's Word, it is because of God and not the reader.

"The Advocate, the Holy Spirit, whom the Father will send in my name, will teach you all things and will remind you of everything I have said to you" (John 14:26).

Before reading the Bible, pray and invite God to speak to you. Don't go to Scripture looking for your idea, but go searching for his.

Not only should you read the Bible prayerfully, but you should also read it carefully. *"Seek and you will find"* is the pledge. The Bible is not a newspaper to be skimmed but rather a mine to be quarried. *"If you look for it as for silver and search for it as for hidden treasure, then you will understand the fear of the LORD and find the knowledge of God"* (Proverbs 2:4–5).

Any worthy find requires effort. The Bible is no exception. To understand the Bible, you don't have to be brilliant, but you must be willing to roll up your sleeves and search.

"Do your best to present yourself to God as one approved, a worker who does not need to be ashamed and who correctly handles the word of truth" (2 Timothy 2:15).

Here's a practical point. Study the Bible a bit at a time. Hunger is not satisfied by eating twenty-one meals in one sitting once a week. The body needs a steady diet to remain strong. So does the soul. When God sent food to his people in the wilderness, he didn't provide loaves already made. Instead, he sent them manna in the shape of *"thin flakes like frost on the ground"* (Exodus 16:14).

God gave manna in limited portions.

God sends spiritual food the same way. He opens the heavens with just enough nutrients for today's hunger. He provides *"a rule for this, a rule for that; a little here, a little there"* (Isaiah 28:10).

Don't be discouraged if your reading reaps a small harvest. Some days a lesser portion is all that is needed. What is important is to search every day for that day's message. A steady diet of God's Word over a lifetime builds a healthy soul and mind.

It's much like the little girl who returned from her first day at school feeling a bit dejected. Her mom asked, "Did you learn anything?"

"Apparently not enough," the girl responded. "I have to go back tomorrow, and the next day, and the next . . . "

Such is the case with learning. And such is the case with Bible study. Understanding comes little by little over a lifetime.

There is a third step in understanding the Bible. After the asking and seeking comes the knocking. After you ask and search, *"knock and the door will be opened to you"* (Matthew 7:7).

To knock is to stand at God's door. To make yourself available. To climb the steps, cross the porch, stand at the doorway, and volunteer. Knocking goes beyond the realm of thinking and into the realm of acting.

To knock is to ask, *What can I do? How can I obey? Where can I go?*

It's one thing to know what to do. It's another to do it. But for those who do it—those who choose to obey—a special reward awaits them.

"Whoever looks intently into the perfect law that gives freedom, and continues in it—not forgetting what they have heard, but doing it—they will be blessed in what they do" (James 1:25).

What a promise. Blessings come to those who do what they read in God's Word! It's the same with medicine. If you only read the label but ignore the pills, it won't help. It's the same with food. If you only read the recipe but never cook, you won't be fed. And it's the same with the Bible. If you only read the words but never obey, you'll never know the joy God has promised.

Ask. Search. Knock. Simple, isn't it? So why don't you give it a try? If you do, you'll see why the Bible is the most remarkable book in history.

INTRODUCTION TO
The Book of Philippians

In an era marked by frustration, could you use more contentment? In a world filled with anxieties, worries, and fears, could you stand to have a bit more joy?

Come with me back in history a couple of thousand years. We're headed for the city of Rome, that thrilling metropolis of gladiators, chariots, and empires. But we won't stop at the coliseum or palace. We'll travel rather to a drab little room surrounded by high walls. We'll imagine we can peek into the room. There we'll see a man seated on the floor. He's an older fellow, balding, with shoulders stooped. Chains encircle his hands and feet. And chained to him is a burly Roman guard.

This is the apostle Paul. The tireless church planter who has traveled all over the world. The preacher who has liberated people in every port. The servant of God bound only by the will of God is now in chains—stuck in a dingy house—attached to a Roman officer.

Surely this is a fellow who has every reason to be in a slump!

He is restricted by walls and is "in chains" (Philippians 1:13). He is afflicted by those who want to "stir up trouble" (verse 17). He is conflicted by the dangers he is facing—"For to me, to live is Christ and to die is gain" (verse 21).

Look closely. He appears to be writing a letter. No doubt it is a complaint letter to God. No doubt it is a list of grievances. No doubt he is writing the New Testament version of Lamentations. After all, he has every reason to be bitter and to complain. But Paul isn't writing such a letter . . . and he doesn't complain. Instead, he writes a letter that 2,000 years later is still known as a treatise on contentment.

Sound interesting? Of course it does. Who couldn't use a guide to joy in this world? Let's follow Paul as he guides us down the trail to unearthly joy and otherworldly peace.

AUTHOR AND DATE

Paul, who persecuted the early church before his life was radically altered by meeting the risen Jesus on the road to Damascus (see Acts 9:1–31). The church at Philippi, located in the Roman province of Macedonia, was the first congregation Paul founded in Europe during his second missionary journey c. AD 50 (see 16:6–15). Paul and Silas were beaten and imprisoned there, but God miraculously sent an earthquake to open the prison doors. After leading the jailer to Christ, they departed for Thessalonica (see 16:16–40). Paul likely wrote the letter c. AD 60 from Rome, where he was imprisoned at the time. It was delivered by Epaphroditus, who had come to Paul at some personal risk with financial help from the church (see Philippians 2:25–30).

SITUATION

Paul had three purposes for writing the letter of Philippians. First, he wanted to acknowledge the believers' gift to him and express his joy in their continued partnership in sharing the gospel of Christ. Second, Paul wanted to explain the purpose and significance of his imprisonment—as it appears the Philippian believers were discouraged to hear of this latest development. Third, Paul wished to address the issues of disunity that Epaphroditus had informed him were arising in the church among the believers. Paul repeatedly encourages them to model Christ's example and try to see things eye-to-eye so peace and harmony will prevail in their fellowship.

KEY THEMES

- By faith we have Christ in us because of the Spirit of God.
- Only Christ can bring salvation.
- Christian unity encourages our faith.

KEY VERSES

In your relationships with one another, have the same mindset as Christ Jesus: who, being in very nature God, did not consider equality with God something to be used to his own advantage (Philippians 2:5–6).

CONTENTS

PRAYING FOR OTHERS

In all my prayers for all of you, I always pray with joy because of your partnership in the gospel from the first day until now.
PHILIPPIANS 1:4–5

REFLECTION

Prayer. You hear sermons about it. You might talk about it with people at church. Perhaps you even read books about it. But when it comes to conversing with God, one on one, what are your actual habits? How much time do you spend in an average day actually talking to the Lord?

_____

_____

_____

_____

SITUATION

Paul generally begins his letters with an expression of thanksgiving for the recipients. However, his letter to the Philippians is unique in that he emphasizes the believers' partnership with him in *sharing* the gospel and expresses his confidence that this continuing partnership—in spite of the fact he is in chains—will culminate as God intends when they stand together before Christ. Paul clearly has a deep affection for this Macedonian congregation, which he demonstrates through his faithfulness in prayer for them.

OBSERVATION

*Read Philippians 1:1–11 from the New International
Version or the New King James Version.*

NEW INTERNATIONAL VERSION
¹ Paul and Timothy, servants of Christ Jesus,

To all God's holy people in Christ Jesus at Philippi, together with the overseers and deacons:

[2] Grace and peace to you from God our Father and the Lord Jesus Christ.

[3] I thank my God every time I remember you. [4] In all my prayers for all of you, I always pray with joy [5] because of your partnership in the gospel from the first day until now, [6] being confident of this, that he who began a good work in you will carry it on to completion until the day of Christ Jesus.

[7] It is right for me to feel this way about all of you, since I have you in my heart and, whether I am in chains or defending and confirming the gospel, all of you share in God's grace with me. [8] God can testify how I long for all of you with the affection of Christ Jesus.

[9] And this is my prayer: that your love may abound more and more in knowledge and depth of insight, [10] so that you may be able to discern what is best and may be pure and blameless for the day of Christ, [11] filled with the fruit of righteousness that comes through Jesus Christ—to the glory and praise of God.

New King James Version

[1] Paul and Timothy, bondservants of Jesus Christ,

To all the saints in Christ Jesus who are in Philippi, with the bishops and deacons:

[2] Grace to you and peace from God our Father and the Lord Jesus Christ.

[3] I thank my God upon every remembrance of you, [4] always in every prayer of mine making request for you all with joy, [5] for your fellowship in the gospel from the first day until now, [6] being confident of this very thing, that He who has begun a good work in you will complete it until the day of Jesus Christ; [7] just as it is right for me to think this of you all, because I have you in my heart, inasmuch as both in my chains and in the defense and confirmation of the gospel, you all are partakers with me of grace. [8] For God is my witness, how greatly I long for you all with the affection of Jesus Christ.

[9] And this I pray, that your love may abound still more and more in knowledge and all discernment, [10] that you may approve the things that are excellent, that you may be sincere and without offense till the day of Christ, [11] being filled with the fruits of righteousness which are by Jesus Christ, to the glory and praise of God.

EXPLORATION

1. What are some of the reasons Paul gives for why he is thankful for the Philippian believers?

_____

_____

_____

_____

_____

2. What is Paul confident of regarding them? What promise does this hold for all believers?

_____

_____

_____

_____

_____

3. What descriptive words does Paul use to describe his attitude for the church in Philippi?

_____

_____

_____

_____

_____

4. What specific requests did Paul bring before God when he prayed for the Philippians?

_____

_____

_____

_____

_____

5. How does Paul's prayer compare to the ones you tend to pray?

_____

_____

_____

_____

6. How does increasing in knowledge and insight help in your spiritual growth?

_____

_____

_____

_____

INSPIRATION

I'd like you to think about someone. His name is not important. His looks are immaterial. His gender is of no concern. His title is irrelevant. He is important not because of who he is, but because of what he did.

He went to Jesus on behalf of a friend. His friend was sick, and Jesus could help, and someone needed to go to Jesus, so someone went. Others cared for the sick man in other ways. Some brought food, others provided treatment, still others comforted the family. Each role was crucial. Each person was helpful, but none was more vital than the one who went to Jesus.

He went because he was asked to go. An earnest appeal came from the family of the afflicted. "We need someone who will tell Jesus that my brother is sick. We need someone to ask him to come. Will you go?"

The question came from two sisters. They would have gone themselves, but they couldn't leave their brother's bedside. They needed someone else to go for them. Not just anyone, mind you, for not just anyone could. Some were too busy, others didn't know the way. Some fatigued too quickly, others were inexperienced on the path. Not everyone could go.

And not everyone would go. This was no small request the sisters were making. They needed a diligent ambassador, someone who knew how to find Jesus. Someone who wouldn't quit mid-journey. Someone who would make sure the message was delivered. Someone who was as convinced as they were that Jesus *must* know what had happened.

They knew of a trustworthy person, and to that person they went. They entrusted their needs to someone, and that someone took those needs to Christ. "So Mary and Martha sent *someone* to tell Jesus, 'Lord, the one you love is sick'" (John 11:3 NCV).

Someone carried the request. Someone walked the trail. Someone went to Jesus on behalf of Lazarus. And because someone went, Jesus responded. (From *The Great House of God* by Max Lucado.)

REACTION

7. How would you describe your willingness to carry out requests for others when asked?

_____

_____

_____

_____

_____

8. How faithful are you in praying for others when they request such spiritual support?

_____

_____

_____

_____

_____

9. If you were to receive a letter from the apostle Paul today, which of your qualities or habits do you think he would praise?

10. In what areas of your life do you need greater spiritual insight and discernment?

11. What elements from Paul's prayer do you need to incorporate more into your life?

12. Who is a Christian friend or relative you could write a short note or email to today for the purpose of providing encouragement?

_____

_____

_____

_____

_____

_____

LIFE LESSONS

Someone observed that joy is found in focusing on Jesus first, others second, and ourselves last. These were Paul's priorities, so it's no wonder he could write such an upbeat epistle even when he was incarcerated! Paul begins his letter with an excited, Christ-centered description of his habits of intercession. As he talks to the Lord about his Macedonian friends, he not only remembers their past acts of love with thanksgiving but also requests heavenly wisdom for their worldly struggles. Furthermore, he looks ahead confidently to their certain maturity. Paul prays with faith and assures the believers of his spiritual support. The result is a contagious joy—for both them and for him. As King David wrote to the Lord, "You will fill me with joy in your presence, with eternal pleasures at your right hand" (Psalm 16:11).

DEVOTION

Father, thank you for the reminder that we can pray for others no matter where we are and no matter what our circumstances are. Help us to develop a more consistent ministry of interceding for our family members, friends, coworkers, and neighbors. Give us joy as we pray—and let us always see prayer as a privilege and not a duty.

JOURNALING

What are specific areas of spiritual growth you would like to see God make in your family members? How will you pray for God to bring about these changes in his way and his timing?

FOR FURTHER READING

To complete the book of Philippians during this twelve-part study, read Philippians 1:1–11. For more Bible passages on intercessory prayer, read Numbers 14:1–24; Nehemiah 1:1–10; Matthew 18:19–20; John 16:23–24; Ephesians 1:15–23; and James 5:13–16.

TRIUMPH IN TROUBLE

But I want you to know, brethren, that the things which happened to me have actually turned out for the furtherance of the gospel, so that it has become evident . . . my chains are in Christ.
PHILIPPIANS 1:12–13 NKJV

REFLECTION

Control is a big deal to most people. We like to have our schedules planned out ahead of time so we can know what we want to accomplish each day. But how do you typically respond when life doesn't cooperate with your plans?

SITUATION

The believers in Philippi had learned Paul was in prison, and it is clear from the apostle's next words that many in the church had become discouraged at this apparent setback. However, Paul reminds the believers that even though *he* might be stuck in a Roman prison, God is still sovereign and at work in the world, orchestrating events to bring about the execution of his perfect will. Paul seeks here to deflect the attention from his own plight and encourage the Philippian believers that his imprisonment has actually served to *advance* the gospel of Christ.

OBSERVATION

*Read Philippians 1:12–18 from the
New International Version or the
New King James Version.*

NEW INTERNATIONAL VERSION

[12] Now I want you to know, brothers and sisters, that what has happened to me has actually served to advance the gospel. [13] As a result, it has become clear throughout the whole palace guard and to everyone else that I am in chains for Christ. [14] And because of my chains, most of the brothers and sisters have become confident in the Lord and dare all the more to proclaim the gospel without fear.

[15] It is true that some preach Christ out of envy and rivalry, but others out of goodwill. [16] The latter do so out of love, knowing that I am put here for the defense of the gospel. [17] The former preach Christ out of selfish ambition, not sincerely, supposing that they can stir up trouble for me while I am in chains. [18] But what does it matter? The important thing is that in every way, whether from false motives or true, Christ is preached. And because of this I rejoice.

Yes, and I will continue to rejoice.

NEW KING JAMES VERSION

[12] But I want you to know, brethren, that the things which happened to me have actually turned out for the furtherance of the gospel, [13] so that it has become evident to the whole palace guard, and to all the rest, that my chains are in Christ; [14] and most of the brethren in the Lord, having become confident by my chains, are much more bold to speak the word without fear.

[15] Some indeed preach Christ even from envy and strife, and some also from goodwill: [16] The former preach Christ from selfish ambition, not sincerely, supposing to add affliction to my chains; [17] but the latter out of love, knowing that I am appointed for the defense of the gospel.

[18] What then? Only that in every way, whether in pretense or in truth, Christ is preached; and in this I rejoice, yes, and will rejoice.

EXPLORATION

1. Paul was a man of action—a missionary church planter. How hard do you think it was for him to adjust to life behind bars (or at least in chains when under house arrest)?

2. How does Paul say his imprisonment has actually turned into a positive situation?

3. What was the effect of Paul's imprisonment on other believers?

4. Why didn't Paul care if some people preached about Christ out of envy or rivalry?

5. Paul refused to dwell on the negative aspects of his situation. How do you think a person develops this habit?

6. What bad situations are present in your life right now? How does this passage help you to view those situations?

INSPIRATION

In the treatment of anxiety, a proper understanding of sovereignty is huge. Anxiety is often the consequence of perceived chaos. If we sense we are victims of unseen, turbulent, random forces, we are troubled. . . .

That's why the most stressed-out people are control freaks. They fail at the quest they most pursue. The more they try to control the world, the more they realize they cannot. Life becomes a cycle of anxiety, failure; anxiety, failure; anxiety, failure. We can't take control, because control is not ours to take.

The Bible has a better idea. Rather than seeking total control, relinquish it. You can't run the world, but you can entrust it to God. This is the message behind Paul's admonition to "rejoice in the Lord." Peace is within reach, not for lack of problems, but because of the presence of a sovereign Lord.

Rather than rehearse the chaos of the world, we can rejoice in the Lord's sovereignty, as Paul did. "Now I want you to know, brothers and sisters, that what has happened to me has actually served to advance the gospel. As a result, it has become clear throughout the whole palace guard and to everyone else that I am in chains for Christ" (Philippians 1:12–13).

And those troublemakers in the church? Those who preached out of "envy and rivalry" (verse 15)? Their selfish motives were no match for the sovereignty of Jesus. "Whether their motives are false or genuine, the message about Christ is being preached either way, so I rejoice. And I will continue to rejoice" (Philippians 1:18 NLT).

To read Paul is to read the words of a man who, in the innermost part of his being, believed in the steady hand of a good God. He was protected by God's strength, preserved by God's love. He lived beneath the shadow of God's wings. Do you?

Stabilize your soul with the sovereignty of God. He reigns supreme over every detail of the universe. "There is no wisdom, no insight, no plan that can succeed against the LORD" (Proverbs 21:30). . . . He sustains "all things by his powerful word" (Hebrews 1:3). He can "whistle for flies from the Nile delta in Egypt" (Isaiah 7:18). He names the stars and knows the sparrows. Great and small, from the People's Liberation Army of China to the army ants in my backyard, everything is under his control. "Who can speak and have it happen if the Lord has not decreed it?

Is it not from the mouth of the Most High that both calamities and good things come?" (Lamentations 3:37–38).

God's answer for troubled times has always been the same: heaven has an occupied throne. (From *Anxious for Nothing* by Max Lucado.)

REACTION

7. How does understanding God's sovereignty help you to view seemingly out-of-control situations in your life?

8. How might God be wanting to work through the bad situations in your life just now for his glory and your good?

9. In what areas of your life do you need to completely relinquish control to God?

10. Paul provides good principle in this passage about the possible wrong motives of others. What are some common wrong motives that Christians have for praying, witnessing to others, attending worship, giving to others, and the like?

_____

_____

_____

11. Paul was passionate about advancing the gospel of Christ. What would those who know you best say is your driving desire in life?

_____

_____

_____

12. When you look at how you tend to respond to adversity, would you say your example is an encouragement or discouragement to others? Why?

_____

_____

_____

LIFE LESSONS

Let's be honest . . . _control_ is an illusion. We can't engineer our own problem-free lives, and we can't make others live the way we want them to live. About the only thing we can control is our response to situations. Will we look for God in the midst of trouble? Will we trust he is at work? Will we keep doing right no matter what? Paul is a great role model for us. He absolutely refused to pursue his own agenda because he saw himself as a mere servant of Christ. He made plans, but he held them in an open hand. When hard times came, his response wasn't to pout but to yield to God's authority by humbly saying, "Your will be done."

DEVOTION

Lord, we are often guilty of desiring our own will more than your plans and purposes. As a result, we get frustrated when things don't go our way. Teach us the art of surrendering to your bigger and better purposes. Show us how to experience triumph even in times of trouble.

JOURNALING

Review a past trial or hardship you experienced. What are some positives that came from it?

FOR FURTHER READING

To complete the book of Philippians during this twelve-part study, read Philippians 1:12–18. For more Bible passages on experiencing triumph in trouble, read Genesis 45:1–13; 50:15– 21; Isaiah 14:24–27; 55:8–9; Daniel 3:8–27; and Luke 24:1–8.

LESSON THREE

STANDING FIRM

*Stand firm in the one Spirit, striving together
as one for the faith of the gospel without being
frightened in any way by those who oppose you.
This is a sign to them that they will be destroyed,
but that you will be saved—and that by God.*

PHILIPPIANS 1:27–28

REFLECTION

There has rarely been a time in the last 2,000 years when Christians haven't been ridiculed and criticized in some way by people. What are some of the most common complaints against believers? Which of these attacks, if any, would you say are legitimate?

SITUATION

Paul's most important goal in life was for the gospel to be proclaimed throughout the world. It didn't matter to him if the motives of the people sharing that message were for envy, or rivalry, or even for love and good-will. It also didn't matter if he was the one delivering the message—he would continue to rejoice in spite of any hardships or setbacks because he knew God was always in control. In this next section, Paul builds on this encouragement to the Philippian believers by making an appeal for them to live with a steadfast unity, for he knows that this will serve to achieve this same purpose of attracting others to the gospel of Christ.

OBSERVATION

Read Philippians 1:19–30 from the New International Version or the New King James Version.

NEW INTERNATIONAL VERSION

[19] For I know that through your prayers and God's provision of the Spirit of Jesus Christ what has happened to me will turn out for my deliverance. [20] I eagerly expect and hope that I will in no way be ashamed, but will have sufficient courage so that now as always Christ will be exalted in my body, whether by life or by death. [21] For to me, to live is Christ and to die is gain. [22] If I am to go on living in the body, this will mean fruitful labor for me. Yet what shall I choose? I do not know! [23] I am torn between the two: I desire to depart and be with Christ, which is better by far; [24] but it is more necessary for you that I remain in the body. [25] Convinced of this, I know that I will remain, and I will continue with all of you for your progress and joy in the faith, [26] so that through my being with you again your boasting in Christ Jesus will abound on account of me.

[27] Whatever happens, conduct yourselves in a manner worthy of the gospel of Christ. Then, whether I come and see you or only hear about you in my absence, I will know that you stand firm in the one Spirit, striving together as one for the faith of the gospel [28] without being frightened in any way by those who oppose you. This is a sign to them that they will be destroyed, but that you will be saved—and that by God. [29] For it has been granted to you on behalf of Christ not only to believe in him, but also to suffer for him, [30] since you are going through the same struggle you saw I had, and now hear that I still have.

NEW KING JAMES VERSION

[19] For I know that this will turn out for my deliverance through your prayer and the supply of the Spirit of Jesus Christ, [20] according to my earnest expectation and hope that in nothing I shall be ashamed, but with all boldness, as always, so now also Christ will be magnified in my

body, whether by life or by death. ²¹ For to me, to live is Christ, and to die is gain. ²² But if I live on in the flesh, this will mean fruit from my labor; yet what I shall choose I cannot tell. ²³ For I am hard-pressed between the two, having a desire to depart and be with Christ, which is far better. ²⁴ Nevertheless to remain in the flesh is more needful for you. ²⁵ And being confident of this, I know that I shall remain and continue with you all for your progress and joy of faith, ²⁶ that your rejoicing for me may be more abundant in Jesus Christ by my coming to you again.

²⁷ Only let your conduct be worthy of the gospel of Christ, so that whether I come and see you or am absent, I may hear of your affairs, that you stand fast in one spirit, with one mind striving together for the faith of the gospel, ²⁸ and not in any way terrified by your adversaries, which is to them a proof of perdition, but to you of salvation, and that from God. ²⁹ For to you it has been granted on behalf of Christ, not only to believe in Him, but also to suffer for His sake, ³⁰ having the same conflict which you saw in me and now hear is in me.

EXPLORATION

1. Why did Paul say he could continue to rejoice in spite of his suffering and imprisonment?

_____

_____

_____

_____

_____

2. What did Paul mean when he said "to live is Christ and to die is gain" (Philippians 1:21)?

_____

_____

_____

_____

3. What are some actions that you would consider worthy of the gospel of Christ?

4. Why is it often difficult for believers to stand "stand firm in the one Spirit" (verse 27)?

5. Paul's only real concern for the Philippians was a lack of unity. What factors pose the most dangerous threat to the harmony of a local church?

6. According to Paul, what behavior contributes to fearlessness among believers?

INSPIRATION

"Hallowed be Your Name" (Matthew 6:9 NKJV). The phrase in Jesus' prayer is a petition, not a proclamation. A request, not an announcement. "Hallowed *be* Your name . . . do whatever it takes to be holy in my life. Take your rightful place on the throne. Exalt yourself. Magnify yourself. Glorify yourself. You be Lord, and I'll be quiet."

The word *hallowed* comes from the word *holy,* and the word *holy* means "to separate." The ancestry of the term can be traced back to an ancient word which means "to cut." To be holy, then, is to be a cut above the norm, superior, extra-ordinary. Remember . . . the Holy One dwells on a different level from the rest of us. What frightens us does not frighten him. What troubles us does not trouble him.

I'm more a landlubber than a sailor, but I've puttered around in a bass boat enough to know the secret for finding land in a storm . . . You don't aim at another boat. You certainly don't stare at the waves. You set your sights on an object unaffected by the wind—a light on the shore—and go straight toward it. The light is unaffected by the storm.

By seeking God . . . you do the same. When you set your sights on our God, you focus on the one "a cut above" any storm life may bring. (From *The Great House of God* by Max Lucado.)

REACTION

7. What are some ways that believers in Christ live "hallowed" or "separate" lives for God?

---

8. Why is it critical to wholeheartedly pray, "Lord, do whatever it takes to be holy in my life"?

9. What role does the Holy Spirit play in helping preserve unity among God's people?

10. The reality is that people are watching your behavior as a Christian —and this can either persuade or dissuade them from seeking Jesus. What would you say is your reputation as a Christian? What about your church's reputation?

11. Paul challenged the Philippian believers to strive "together for the faith of the gospel" (verse 27). What would this look like in the life of your church or small group?

12. When have you struggled or suffered most as a Christian? What helped to get you through that particular time in your life?

LIFE LESSONS

As Jesus' earthly life and ministry drew to a close, he spoke urgently and prayed fervently about the unified way his followers should live. In short, Christ wants us to live in harmony (see John 17:11) and love one another sacrificially (see 13:34–35). Such unconditional devotion sets us apart and causes the world to stare in awe. Conversely, when we bicker and feud among ourselves, when churches split, or when we bring shame on the name of Christ, the world mocks. It is only in unity we shine and only together we fully enjoy all the blessings of God. Shared sorrows are halved sorrows. Shared joys are doubled joys. What will you change this week to ensure that all your interactions with other believers are worthy of the gospel?

DEVOTION

Lord Jesus, you deserve to be represented by believers who are holy and who live in harmony with one another. Today, we make the psalmist's prayer our own: "Test me, Lord, and try me, examine my heart and my mind; for I have always been mindful of your unfailing love and have lived in reliance on your faithfulness" (Psalm 26:2). Show us any actions we need to change.

JOURNALING

What damaged relationships do you have with another Christian that needs attention? What will it take on your part to heal the rift?

FOR FURTHER READING

To complete the book of Philippians during this twelve-part study, read Philippians 1:19–30. For more Bible passages on conduct worthy of Christ, read 1 Corinthians 1:10–17; 2 Corinthians 13:5–11; 1 Timothy 4:11–16; James 3:13–16; 1 Peter 2:11–17; and 2 Peter 3:10–13.

LESSON FOUR

ALL FOR ONE

Fulfill my joy by being like-minded,
having the same love, being of
one accord, of one mind.
Philippians 2:2 NKJV

REFLECTION

Perhaps you've been fortunate to be part of a sports team, congregation, or other organization marked by unusual camaraderie and a deep sense of oneness. What are some factors that brought unity to this group? What were the benefits you witnessed as a result?

_____

_____

_____

_____

SITUATION

Paul has now raised a key matter he wishes to address further with the Philippian believers: the issue of them conducting themselves in a way that will serve to bring others to Christ. Although he is thankful for them, he has undoubtedly heard of some disharmony among the members of the congregation that is disrupting their witness to the world. In this next section, Paul begins to address this concern by pointing out some of the qualities that make for a harmonious and unified community—one that imitates the example and humility of Christ.

OBSERVATION

Read Philippians 2:1–4 from the New International Version or the New King James Version.

New International Version
[1] Therefore if you have any encouragement from being united with Christ, if any comfort from his love, if any common sharing in the Spirit, if any tenderness and compassion, [2] then make my joy complete by being like-minded, having the same love, being one in spirit and of one mind.

³ Do nothing out of selfish ambition or vain conceit. Rather, in humility value others above yourselves, ⁴ not looking to your own interests but each of you to the interests of the others.

New King James Version

¹ Therefore if there is any consolation in Christ, if any comfort of love, if any fellowship of the Spirit, if any affection and mercy, ² fulfill my joy by being like-minded, having the same love, being of one accord, of one mind. ³ Let nothing be done through selfish ambition or conceit, but in lowliness of mind let each esteem others better than himself. ⁴ Let each of you look out not only for his own interests, but also for the interests of others.

EXPLORATION

1. Scholars point out Paul's "if" statements in Philippians 2:1 could be translated "since." In other words, Christians *do* enjoy these advantages. Why are these such important privileges?

_____

_____

_____

2. What are the implications of Paul's claim that the same Spirit of God indwells all believers?

_____

_____

_____

3. How would you define what Paul means by "being like-minded . . . being one in spirit and of one mind" (verse 2)? Give some examples.

_____

_____

_____

4. Why do you think Paul said his joy would be complete if believers acted in this manner?

_____

_____

_____

5. How can you tell if you are being motivated by "selfish ambition or vain conceit" (verse 3)?

_____

_____

_____

6. Why is it often so hard to put the needs and interests of others above your own?

_____

_____

_____

INSPIRATION

Broken people come to churches. Not with broken bones, but with broken hearts, homes, dreams, and lives. They limp in on fractured faith, and if the church operates as the church, they find healing. Pastor-teachers touch and teach. Gospel bearers share good news. Prophets speak words of truth. Visionaries dream of greater impact. Some administer. Some pray. Some lead. Some follow. But all help to heal brokenness: "to make the body of Christ stronger."

My favorite example of this truth involves a man named Randy, an elder in our church. He loves the congregation so much that he smells like the sheep he tends. Between running a business and raising a family, he encourages the sick and calls on the confused. Few men have kinder hearts. And yet, few men have had their hearts put on ice as his was the night his father was murdered and his stepmother was arrested for his death. She was eventually acquitted, but the deed left Randy with no dad, no inheritance, and no answers.

How do you recover from that? Randy will tell you it is through the church. Friends prayed for him, wept with him, stood by him. Finally, after months of wrestling with anger and sorrow, he resolved to move on. The decision came in a moment of worship. God sutured Randy's heart with the lyrics of a hymn. Randy calls it a miracle. That makes two of us.

God heals his family through his family. In the church we use our gifts to love each other, honor one another, keep an eye on troublemakers, and carry each other's burdens. Do you need encouragement, prayers, or a hospitable home? God entrusts the church to purvey these treasures. Consider the church God's treatment center. . . .

Don't miss it. No one is strong all the time. Don't miss the place to find your place and heal your hurts. (From *Cure for the Common Life* by Max Lucado.)

REACTION

7. What does this story tell you about the importance of looking "for the interests of others" (Philippians 2:4)?

_____

_____

_____

8. One of the great claims of the New Testament is that believers are all "in Christ." The phrase occurs eight times in Philippians alone. How should you act when you consider that you are a member of Christ's body (see 1 Corinthians 12:12–31)?

_____

_____

_____

_____

9. Our culture practically worships the ideals of autonomy and individualism. In what ways are these values counterproductive to what God is trying to do in and through his body?

10. What exactly is "lowliness of mind" (verse 3 NKJV)?

11. What are some practical ways Christians can demonstrate humility and give more honor to others than to themselves?

12. How can you develop the kind of mindset that looks first to the interests of others?

LIFE LESSONS

Like it or not, we are walking billboards for the gospel. People form opinions about Christ and draw conclusions about our faith based on how we live and interact. Imagine the damage when we claim to be brand-new people but then hold on to petty grudges. Or when we advertise ourselves as a God-inhabited community, yet our relationships are marked by self-centeredness and divisiveness. Paul suggests such disunity is the result of spiritual immaturity and insecurity. It's only when we truly embrace the infinite resources provided by Christ that we find the capacity to stop our selfish grasping for lesser things. When we are secure in him, we are freed up to become others-centered. Such selflessness shocks the world.

DEVOTION

Father, you have given us all we need to be a jaw-dropping faith community. We are in Christ. We experience the comfort and force of his love. We share life in the Spirit who fills us with mercy and kindness. Now, strengthened by and secure in all these resources, may we let go of our selfish desires and pursue lives of radical servanthood.

JOURNALING

What interests can you list of five significant people in your life? What are some ways you could selflessly put their needs first this week?

FOR FURTHER READING

To complete the book of Philippians during this twelve-part study, read Philippians 2:1–4. For more Bible passages on unity, read Romans 12:3–8; 1 Corinthians 10:14–17; Galatians 3:26–29; Ephesians 4:1–6; and 1 Peter 3:8–9.

ULTIMATE SERVANTHOOD

Christ Jesus . . . being in very nature God, did not consider equality with God something to be used to his own advantage; rather, he made himself nothing by taking the very nature of a servant, being made in human likeness.

PHILIPPIANS 2:5–7

REFLECTION

Think back on the various jobs you have held and the volunteer assignments you have undertaken. Which assignments or responsibilities have been the most menial and humbling to you? Describe one such experience.

SITUATION

In this next section of the letter, Paul continues to expound on the types of characteristics that believers in Christ must adopt in order to live in harmony with one another. To do this, Paul points to the ultimate example of humble servanthood that he can provide: Jesus' decision to put aside his divinity, become a human, and willingly sacrifice his life in obedience to the Father. As Paul notes, it is only through Christ, and only by embracing his attitudes and actions, that we can find true unity and joy.

OBSERVATION

Read Philippians 2:5–11 from the New International
Version or the New King James Version.

NEW INTERNATIONAL VERSION

[5] In your relationships with one another, have the same mindset as Christ Jesus:

> [6] Who, being in very nature God,
>   did not consider equality with God something to be used to
>   his own advantage;
> [7] rather, he made himself nothing
>   by taking the very nature of a servant,
>   being made in human likeness.
> [8] And being found in appearance as a man,
>   he humbled himself
>   by becoming obedient to death—
>   even death on a cross!
> [9] Therefore God exalted him to the highest place
>   and gave him the name that is above every name,
> [10] that at the name of Jesus every knee should bow,
>   in heaven and on earth and under the earth,
> [11] and every tongue acknowledge that Jesus Christ is Lord,
>   to the glory of God the Father.

NEW KING JAMES VERSION

[5] Let this mind be in you which was also in Christ Jesus, [6] who, being in the form of God, did not consider it robbery to be equal with God, [7] but made Himself of no reputation, taking the form of a bondservant, and coming in the likeness of men. [8] And being found in appearance as a man, He humbled Himself and became obedient to the point of death, even the death of the cross. [9] Therefore God also has highly exalted Him

and given Him the name which is above every name, [10] that at the name of Jesus every knee should bow, of those in heaven, and of those on earth, and of those under the earth, [11] and that every tongue should confess that Jesus Christ is Lord, to the glory of God the Father.

EXPLORATION

1. What does it mean to have the "same mindset as Christ Jesus" (Philippians 2:5)?

_____

_____

_____

_____

2. Being a disciple means imitating one's master or teacher in thoughts, actions, and character. Where are your attitudes most like Christ's? Where are they most unlike Jesus' attitudes?

_____

_____

_____

_____

3. Paul notes that Jesus, in taking on full humanity, gave up the advantages of his divinity and "made himself nothing" (verses 7). What are some examples of this you can cite from the Gospels (see, for example, Matthew 4:2; Mark 13:32; John 4:6; 6:38; 11:33–35; and 19:28)?

_____

_____

_____

_____

4. As God's ultimate servant, Jesus always acted in absolute dependence on his Father (see John 5:19; 8:28; and 14:10). What can you learn from this example?

_____

_____

_____

_____

_____

5. Jesus said that he "did not come to be served, but to serve" (Mark 10:45). If you dare to live likewise, how can be assured that your needs will be met?

_____

_____

_____

_____

_____

6. How does God reward those who humble themselves and serve (see Luke 18:14)?

_____

_____

_____

_____

_____

INSPIRATION

Jesus was "in very nature God." Before Bethlehem, Jesus had every advantage and benefit of deity. He was boundless, timeless, and limitless. "All things were made through Him, and without Him nothing was made that was made" (John 1:3 NKJV).

Every rock, tree, and planet needs a stamp that says, "Made by Jesus." He gets credit for the Whirlpool Galaxy. It contains more than a hundred billion stars. He created our sun. More than a million earths could fit inside the sun. Jesus fashioned Betelgeuse, which if it were placed at the center of the earth's solar system, would extend out to the orbit of Jupiter. . . . Jesus spoke and the bespangled sky happened. He calls each star by name and can fold up the skies as a Bedouin would pack his tent.

Paul's headline, however, is not "Christ the Creator." It is, "Christ the Incarnate One." The One who made everything "made himself nothing" (Philippians 2:7). Christ made himself small. He made himself dependent upon lungs, a larynx, and legs. He experienced hunger and thirst. He went through all the normal stages of human development. He was taught to walk, stand, wash his face, and dress himself. His muscles grew stronger; his hair grew longer. His voice cracked when he passed through puberty. He was genuinely human.

When he was "full of joy" (Luke 10:21), his joy was authentic. When he "wept over" Jerusalem (Luke 19:41), his tears were as real as yours or mine. When he asked, "How long must I put up with you?" (Matthew 17:17 NLT), his frustration was honest. When he cried out from the cross, "My God, my God, why have you forsaken me?" (27:46), he needed an answer. He knew only what the Father revealed to him (see John 12:50). If the Father did not give direction, Jesus did not claim to have it.

He took "the very nature of a servant" (Philippians 2:7). He became like us so he could serve us! He entered the world not to demand our allegiance but to display his affection. He did not view his equality with God as "something to be used to his own advantage" (verse 6). He refused to throw his weight around. He divested himself of divine advantage.

When people mocked him, he didn't turn them into stones. When soldiers spat on him, he didn't boomerang their spit. When people called him crazy, he didn't strike them blind. Just the opposite. He became "obedient to death—even death on a cross!" (verse 8).

Paul gave special emphasis: "*even* death on a cross." Crucifixion was the cruelest form of execution in the Roman Empire. It was commonly reserved for those of the lowest class, especially slaves. . . . God took the nails. God took the whips. God bore the shame. God felt the tip of the spear. God exhaled a final breath. Jesus descended the ladder of incarnation one rung at a time. (From *Because of Bethlehem* by Max Lucado.)

REACTION

7. How do you react when you consider all that Jesus gave up to come into this world and sacrifice his life to pay for your sins?

_____

_____

_____

8. Servanthood requires no special training or gifting. Given this, why do you think it is often so rare to see today?

_____

_____

_____

_____

9. What are the key ingredients to a life of servanthood?

_____

_____

_____

_____

10. How would the atmosphere in a church change if it were filled with humble servants?

_____

_____

_____

_____

11. What is it like to work for you or to be under your authority? How do you treat those who serve under you?

_____

_____

_____

12. How can a life of servanthood—giving up your rights, putting others first, refusing to promote yourself—be a path to glory and joy?

_____

_____

_____

LIFE LESSONS

The Father in heaven is not only *with* us but also *in* us. He listens to us. He never abandons us. He cares about us and only wants the best for us. If we truly understand this truth, we recognize that all things are possible. We no longer have to scramble around trying to make life work. We can relax and go "off-duty." We can let go of the joy-depleting habit of looking out for number one. Even better, when we are convinced the Father is absolutely for us, we are freed up to focus all our attention and energy and efforts on living for him by serving others. As surrendered servants, we can rest assured he will meet all our needs.

DEVOTION

Lord Jesus, thank you for your humble sacrifice. You gave your life to give us life. In gratitude, we want to respond today by giving our lives to serve others. Thank you for the assurance that you will supply all our needs as we humbly seek to follow your example.

JOURNALING

What are some tangible acts of servanthood you could engage in this week?

FOR FURTHER READING

To complete the book of Philippians during this twelve-part study, read Philippians 2:5–11. For more Bible passages on humble servanthood, read Micah 6:6–8; Matthew 20:20–28; Luke 14:7–14; 22:24–30; John 13:1–17; James 4:7–10; and 1 Peter 5:5–7.

SHINING FOR CHRIST

*Do all things without complaining and disputing,
that you may become blameless and harmless,
children of God without fault in the midst of
a crooked and perverse generation, among
whom you shine as lights in the world.*
PHILIPPIANS 2:14–15 NKJV

REFLECTION

Like snowflakes and fingerprints, no two Christians are alike. God is working in each of our lives in varied ways and according to a unique blueprint. What are the areas of your life in which you see tangible growth and progress? What are the areas in which you long for change?

SITUATION

Paul has now called the believers in Philippi to put aside their petty differences with one another and look to the example of Christ as their model for how to regard one another. As they consider the depths of Jesus' obedience to the Father for their sake, it should compel them—with "fear and trembling" (Philippians 2:12)—to model a similar type of obedience to God. Just as Christ obeyed, they are to obey without grumbling or arguing. As they do, they will prove themselves to be a light for Jesus to a dark and hurting world.

OBSERVATION

Read Philippians 2:12–18 from the New International Version or the New King James Version.

New International Version

12 Therefore, my dear friends, as you have always obeyed—not only in my presence, but now much more in my absence—continue to work out your

salvation with fear and trembling, [13] for it is God who works in you to will and to act in order to fulfill his good purpose.

[14] Do everything without grumbling or arguing, [15] so that you may become blameless and pure, "children of God without fault in a warped and crooked generation." Then you will shine among them like stars in the sky [16] as you hold firmly to the word of life. And then I will be able to boast on the day of Christ that I did not run or labor in vain. [17] But even if I am being poured out like a drink offering on the sacrifice and service coming from your faith, I am glad and rejoice with all of you. [18] So you too should be glad and rejoice with me.

New King James Version

[12] Therefore, my beloved, as you have always obeyed, not as in my presence only, but now much more in my absence, work out your own salvation with fear and trembling; [13] for it is God who works in you both to will and to do for His good pleasure.

[14] Do all things without complaining and disputing, [15] that you may become blameless and harmless, children of God without fault in the midst of a crooked and perverse generation, among whom you shine as lights in the world, [16] holding fast the word of life, so that I may rejoice in the day of Christ that I have not run in vain or labored in vain.

[17] Yes, and if I am being poured out as a drink offering on the sacrifice and service of your faith, I am glad and rejoice with you all. [18] For the same reason you also be glad and rejoice with me.

EXPLORATION

1. What kind of response should believers have when they consider what Jesus did for them?

_____

_____

_____

_____

2. Go through this brief passage and look at the number of verbs that Paul uses. What particular actions does he expect believers in Christ to do?

_____

_____

_____

_____

3. There is a common tendency for younger Christians to rely on the faith and presence of other believers (see Philippians 2:12). When does spiritual dependence become unhealthy?

_____

_____

_____

_____

4. What is the difference between the biblical command to _work out_ your salvation and the misguided attempt to _work for_ your salvation?

_____

_____

_____

_____

5. How can you live out "the joy of your salvation" (Psalm 51:12) if you are expected to work out your salvation "with fear and trembling? (Philippians 2:12)?

_____

_____

_____

6. How can you avoid the ever-present danger of trying to live an exemplary life so *you* will get the attention and admiration of others? How does this passage help you in this?

_____

_____

_____

_____

INSPIRATION

We applause-aholics have done it all: dropped names, sung loudly, dressed up to look classy, dressed down to look cool, quoted authors we've never read, spouted Greek we've never studied. For the life of me, I believe Satan trains battalions of demons to whisper one question in our ears: "What are people thinking of you?"

A deadly query. What they think of us matters not. What they think of God matters all. God will not share his glory with another (see Isaiah 42:8). Next time you need a nudge away from the spotlight, remember, *You are simply one link in a chain . . . an unimportant link at that.*

Don't agree? Take it up with the apostle Paul. "So neither the one who plants nor the one who waters is anything, but only God, who makes things grow" (1 Corinthians 3:7).

Remember the other messengers God has used? A donkey to speak to Balaam (see Numbers 22:28). A staff-turned-snake to stir Pharaoh (see Exodus 7:10). He even used stubborn oxen to make a point about reverence and a big fish to make a point about reluctant preachers (see 1 Samuel 6:1–12 and Jonah 1:1–17).

God doesn't need you and me to do his work. We are expedient messengers, ambassadors by his kindness, not by our cleverness. It's not about us, and it angers him when we think it is. (From *It's Not About Me* by Max Lucado.)

REACTION

7. As you do good works for Christ, are some signs you might have crossed the line from dwelling on what people are thinking of *your Savior* to what people are thinking of *you*?

_____

_____

_____

_____

8. What qualities do you see in the Bible of the people God used to do great things for him?

_____

_____

_____

_____

_____

9. Why do you think Paul stresses the importance of doing everything without grumbling or arguing? How will you put that into effect in your life this week?

_____

_____

_____

_____

10. What are some of the ways "God is working in you to help you want to do and be able to do what pleases him" (Philippians 2:13 NCV)?

_____

_____

_____

_____

11. What are some actions that would result in your shining more brightly for Christ?

_____

_____

_____

_____

12. What are some ways this week you can "hold firmly to the word of life" (verse 16)—both clinging to it and also offering it to others?

_____

_____

_____

_____

LIFE LESSONS

What does the moon do? It generates no light. Contrary to the lyrics of the old song, the moon cannot "shine on, shine on . . . up in the sky." Apart from the sun, the moon is nothing more than a gray pockmarked rock. But properly positioned, the moon beams. Let it do what it was made to do, and a clod of dirt becomes a source of inspiration and a symbol of romance. The moon reflects the greater light of the sun. What would happen if we also accepted our place as Son reflectors? What if we made it our goal to shine with all the brightness of Christ?

DEVOTION

Lord, we want to make progress in our faith not so that people will notice us but so that they will might marvel at you. We offer you are wills today— make them yours. We offer our weaknesses and request your infinite strength. Shine through us today.

JOURNALING

How have you nurtured a deep sense of reverence for God as you lived your life for Christ?

_____

_____

_____

_____

_____

_____

_____

_____

_____

_____

_____

_____

_____

_____

_____

_____

FOR FURTHER READING

To complete the book of Philippians during this twelve-part study, read Philippians 2:12–18. For more Bible passages on shining the light of Christ, read Isaiah 49:5–6; Daniel 12:1–3; Matthew 5:13–16; John 5:33–36; 8:12–20; Acts 6:12–15; 2 Corinthians 3:12–18; and Ephesians 5:6–10.

LESSON SEVEN

ROLE MODELS

*I have no one else like him, who will
show genuine concern for your welfare.
For everyone looks out for their own
interests, not those of Jesus Christ.*
PHILIPPIANS 2:20–21

REFLECTION

Our culture has its share of celebrities, and often these people are famous for nothing more than being famous! There is, of course, a huge difference between being a character and having character. Who are the people you most admire—especially in the spiritual realm? Why?

_____

_____

_____

_____

SITUATION

Paul has pointed to the example of Christ to compel the Philippian believers to put aside their differences, embrace unity, and obediently follow God in a way that will attract others to the message of salvation. If they do this, Paul states, he will be able to "boast" when his time on this earth is complete that his efforts on their behalf were not in vain. As a further illustration for how he desires the believers to act, Paul draws on the examples of his co-workers Timothy and Epaphroditus, whose conducts serves as role models of faithfulness and selflessness.

OBSERVATION

Read Philippians 2:19–30 from the New International Version or the New King James Version.

NEW INTERNATIONAL VERSION

¹⁹ I hope in the Lord Jesus to send Timothy to you soon, that I also may be cheered when I receive news about you. ²⁰ I have no one else like him,

who will show genuine concern for your welfare. ²¹ For everyone looks out for their own interests, not those of Jesus Christ. ²² But you know that Timothy has proved himself, because as a son with his father he has served with me in the work of the gospel. ²³ I hope, therefore, to send him as soon as I see how things go with me. ²⁴ And I am confident in the Lord that I myself will come soon.

²⁵ But I think it is necessary to send back to you Epaphroditus, my brother, co-worker and fellow soldier, who is also your messenger, whom you sent to take care of my needs. ²⁶ For he longs for all of you and is distressed because you heard he was ill. ²⁷ Indeed he was ill, and almost died. But God had mercy on him, and not on him only but also on me, to spare me sorrow upon sorrow. ²⁸ Therefore I am all the more eager to send him, so that when you see him again you may be glad and I may have less anxiety. ²⁹ So then, welcome him in the Lord with great joy, and honor people like him, ³⁰ because he almost died for the work of Christ. He risked his life to make up for the help you yourselves could not give me.

New King James Version

¹⁹ But I trust in the Lord Jesus to send Timothy to you shortly, that I also may be encouraged when I know your state. ²⁰ For I have no one like-minded, who will sincerely care for your state. ²¹ For all seek their own, not the things which are of Christ Jesus. ²² But you know his proven character, that as a son with his father he served with me in the gospel. ²³ Therefore I hope to send him at once, as soon as I see how it goes with me. ²⁴ But I trust in the Lord that I myself shall also come shortly.

²⁵ Yet I considered it necessary to send to you Epaphroditus, my brother, fellow worker, and fellow soldier, but your messenger and the one who ministered to my need; ²⁶ since he was longing for you all, and was distressed because you had heard that he was sick. ²⁷ For indeed he was sick almost unto death; but God had mercy on him, and not only on him but on me also, lest I should have sorrow upon sorrow. ²⁸ Therefore I sent him the more eagerly, that when you see him again you may rejoice, and I may be less sorrowful. ²⁹ Receive him therefore in the Lord with

all gladness, and hold such men in esteem; [30] because for the work of Christ he came close to death, not regarding his life, to supply what was lacking in your service toward me.

EXPLORATION

1. Why did Paul hold Timothy in such high regard?

_____

_____

_____

2. What are some unique traits that set Timothy apart and made him such an effective partner with Paul in sharing the gospel?

_____

_____

_____

3. What were the outstanding qualities of Epaphroditus?

_____

_____

_____

4. Paul encouraged the Philippians to honor people like Epaphroditus. What does this look like?

_____

_____

_____

5. We tend to place the people mentioned in Scripture on a pedestal. Why would this serve as a disservice to them and to you?

_____

_____

_____

6. Why did Paul call out the example of these two men? How do they serve as practical examples of humility and service to the believers in Philippi?

_____

_____

_____

INSPIRATION

The church of Jesus Christ began with a group of frightened men in a second-floor room in Jerusalem.

Though trained and taught, they didn't know what to say. Though they'd marched with him for three years, they now sat . . . afraid. They were timid soldiers, reluctant warriors, speechless messengers.

Their most courageous act was to get up and lock the door.

Some looked out the window, some looked at the wall, some looked at the floor, but all looked inside themselves.

And well they should, for it was an hour of self-examination. All their efforts seemed so futile. Nagging their memories were the promises they'd made but not kept. When the Roman soldiers took Jesus, Jesus' followers took off. With the very wine of the covenant on their breath and the bread of his sacrifice in their bellies, they fled.

All those boasts of bravado? All those declarations of devotion? They lay broken and shattered at the gate of Gethsemane's garden.

We don't know where the disciples went when they fled the garden, but we do know what they took: a memory. They took a heart-stopping memory of a man who called himself no less than God in the flesh. And they couldn't get him out of their minds.

Try as they might to lose him in the crowd, they couldn't forget him. If they saw a leper, they thought of his compassion. If they heard a storm, they would remember the day he silenced one. If they saw a child, they would think of the day he held one. And if they saw a lamb being carried to the temple, they would remember his face streaked with blood and his eyes flooded with love.

No, they couldn't forget him. As a result, they came back. And, as a result, the church of our Lord began with a group of frightened men in an upper room. Sound familiar? Things haven't changed much in 2,000 years, have they? How many churches today find themselves paralyzed in the upper room? (From *Six Hours One Friday* by Max Lucado.)

REACTION

7. How does it encourage you to realize the "great saints" of the Bible were fallible and fearful and sometimes fickle and faithless?

_____

_____

_____

8. How does it challenge you to watch ordinary people like Timothy and Epaphroditus live extraordinary lives of sacrifice and courage?

_____

_____

_____

9. How can you, like Timothy, develop the godly quality of not just looking out for your own interests?

_____

_____

_____

10. If your spiritual leaders were to describe you, what words and phrases would they use?

_____

_____

_____

11. Epaphroditus risked his life in some way to serve the Philippians. What are some lesser—but still important—risks you can take for Christ this week?

_____

_____

_____

12. How will you demonstrate humility and service to other believers this week?

_____

_____

_____

_____

LIFE LESSONS

Dependable people are like diamonds. They are precious because they are so rare. Experience and know-how are great assets, but they're not much good without trustworthiness. Talent is wonderful, but by itself it's not enough. Far better to be a faithful Christian. Are you? Like Timothy and Epaphroditus, are you a role model for others? Determine to be a person whom others can rely on. Keep your word. Show up. Be consistent. Live for others. Take risks. Be a "go to" guy or gal. Make it your goal, by God's grace, to exemplify a life of spiritual steadiness.

DEVOTION

Father, you have surrounded us with men and women who love you and who model what it means to walk with you. We praise you for the wonderful examples of godliness you have given to us. Show us creative ways to honor our spiritual mentors. And work in our hearts so that more and more we become that kind of role model for others.

JOURNALING

What are some words of appreciation and encouragement you can offer to someone who has been a hero and inspiration in your life? (Be sure to share these thoughts with the person!)

FOR FURTHER READING

To complete the book of Philippians during this twelve-part study, read Philippians 2:19–30. For more Bible passages on spiritual role models, read Proverbs 1:8–19; John 13:12–17; 1 Corinthians 10:31–11:1; 2 Thessalonians 3:6–10; 1 Timothy 4:11–14; and Titus 2:6–8.

RIGHT STANDING WITH GOD

*But what things were gain to me, these
I have counted loss for Christ.*
PHILIPPIANS 3:7 NKJV

REFLECTION

Take a few minutes to compose a brief spiritual résumé. Don't be bashful. What are your spiritual gifts and your God-given abilities? What are some of your most meaningful spiritual experiences? How would you summarize your goals and objectives?

SITUATION

Paul has previously stated that if the believers in Philippi are able to follow the example of Jesus and unite with one another in humility, he will be able to "boast on the day Christ" that he "did not run or labor in vain" (Philippians 2:16). For Paul, any such "boasting" or confidence that believers have in their relationship with God is based solely on the work of Christ, and not on any acts or works that we have done. As support for this claim, Paul draws on the example of his own former life as a Pharisee to show how rigid adherence to the law does not result in righteousness. We are saved by grace—and life the Christian life by grace through faith.

OBSERVATION

Read Philippians 3:1–11 from the New International
Version or the New King James Version.

NEW INTERNATIONAL VERSION

¹ Further, my brothers and sisters, rejoice in the Lord! It is no trouble for me to write the same things to you again, and it is a safeguard for you. ² Watch out for those dogs, those evildoers, those mutilators of the flesh. ³ For it is we who are the circumcision, we who serve God by his Spirit, who boast in Christ Jesus, and who put no confidence in the flesh— ⁴ though I myself have reasons for such confidence.

If someone else thinks they have reasons to put confidence in the flesh, I have more: ⁵ circumcised on the eighth day, of the people of Israel, of the tribe of Benjamin, a Hebrew of Hebrews; in regard to the law, a Pharisee; ⁶ as for zeal, persecuting the church; as for righteousness based on the law, faultless.

⁷ But whatever were gains to me I now consider loss for the sake of Christ. ⁸ What is more, I consider everything a loss because of the surpassing worth of knowing Christ Jesus my Lord, for whose sake I have lost all things. I consider them garbage, that I may gain Christ ⁹ and be found in him, not having a righteousness of my own that comes from the law, but that which is through faith in Christ—the righteousness that comes from God on the basis of faith. ¹⁰ I want to know Christ—yes, to know the power of his resurrection and participation in his sufferings, becoming like him in his death, ¹¹ and so, somehow, attaining to the resurrection from the dead.

NEW KING JAMES VERSION

¹ Finally, my brethren, rejoice in the Lord. For me to write the same things to you is not tedious, but for you it is safe.

² Beware of dogs, beware of evil workers, beware of the mutilation! ³ For we are the circumcision, who worship God in the Spirit, rejoice in

Christ Jesus, and have no confidence in the flesh, [4] though I also might have confidence in the flesh. If anyone else thinks he may have confidence in the flesh, I more so: [5] circumcised the eighth day, of the stock of Israel, of the tribe of Benjamin, a Hebrew of the Hebrews; concerning the law, a Pharisee; [6] concerning zeal, persecuting the church; concerning the righteousness which is in the law, blameless.

[7] But what things were gain to me, these I have counted loss for Christ. [8] Yet indeed I also count all things loss for the excellence of the knowledge of Christ Jesus my Lord, for whom I have suffered the loss of all things, and count them as rubbish, that I may gain Christ [9] and be found in Him, not having my own righteousness, which is from the law, but that which is through faith in Christ, the righteousness which is from God by faith; [10] that I may know Him and the power of His resurrection, and the fellowship of His sufferings, being conformed to His death, [11] if, by any means, I may attain to the resurrection from the dead.

EXPLORATION

1. How does Paul indicate joy is a choice rather than a feeling that comes and goes?

_____

_____

_____

_____

2. The so-called "Judaizers" were trying to get Gentile converts to submit to the Jewish rite of circumcision and other legalistic rituals in order to be saved. Why did this bother Paul?

_____

_____

_____

3. What was Paul's purpose for sharing his impressive spiritual résumé as a devout Jew?

_____

_____

_____

_____

4. How does Paul describe the monumental change that took place in his own religious attitudes and actions after meeting Christ?

_____

_____

_____

_____

5. What is the difference between trying to adhere to a religious system and trusting in the person of Christ?

_____

_____

_____

6. Why do you think Paul said he wanted to participate in Jesus' sufferings? What had he learned during the course of his life about what it meant to truly follow Christ?

_____

_____

_____

INSPIRATION

Paul had blood on his hands and religious diplomas on his wall. But then came the Damascus road moment. Jesus appeared. And once Paul saw Jesus, he couldn't see anymore.

He couldn't see value in his résumé anymore. He couldn't see merit in his merits or worth in his good works anymore. He couldn't see reasons to boast about anything he had done anymore. And he couldn't see any option except to spend the rest of his life talking less about himself and more about Jesus.

He became the great poet of grace. "I once thought these things were valuable, but now I consider them worthless because of what Christ has done" (Philippians 3:7 NLT). In exchange for self-salvation, God gave Paul righteousness. "I no longer count on my own righteousness through obeying the law; rather, I become righteous through faith in Christ. For God's way of making us right with himself depends on faith" (verse 9 NLT). Paul gave his guilt to Jesus. Period. He didn't numb it, hide it, deny it, offset it, or punish it. He simply surrendered it to Jesus. . . .

What would the apostle say to a guilt-laden teenager? Simply this: "Rejoice in the Lord's mercy. Trust in his ability to forgive. Abandon any attempt at self-salvation or justification. No more hiding behind fig leaves. Cast yourself upon the grace of Christ and Christ alone."

A happy saint is one who is at the same time aware of the severity of sin and the immensity of grace. Sin is not diminished, nor is God's ability to forgive it. The saint dwells in grace, not guilt. This is the tranquil soul. (From *Anxious for Nothing* by Max Lucado.)

REACTION

7. Paul was blinded on the road to Damascus after meeting Christ (see Acts 9:8–9). But how did this encounter serve to remove his *spiritual* blindness?

----

8. Paul speaks of formerly having "confidence in the flesh" (Philippians 3:3–4). What exactly does he mean by this phrase?

9. Paul says that because of Christ, the values and practices that were previously so important to him are now like "rubbish" or "garbage" (verse 8). How has this been your experience?

10. Paul's one great passion in life was to know Christ. How does one actually practice this?

11. How can you help your fellow believers in Christ understand that right standing with God doesn't depend on what we do but on what Christ has done on our behalf?

12. Paul not only longed for the power of Christ but also wanted to share in his sufferings. What does it mean to become like Christ in his death (see verse 10)?

_____

_____

_____

_____

_____

_____

LIFE LESSONS

Remember the story Jesus told in Luke 18:9–14 about two men who went into the temple to pray? He described the first man, a Pharisee, as praying "with himself" (verse 11 NKJV). Interesting. This proud man proceeded to rattle off all his religious achievements. It was less a prayer and more a self-congratulatory speech! Meanwhile, the other man, a dishonest tax collector, stood at a distance. Broken. Very much in touch with his own unworthiness. He humbly cried out to God for mercy. And how did heaven respond? Only the tax collector left the temple on right terms with God. Here in this short story is the simple gospel. We are made right with God not by our own efforts, but by simply relying on God's grace.

DEVOTION

Father, thank you for the powerful reminder that salvation is a free gift. We can't earn it or deserve it. We can only receive it. Like Paul, give us an all-consuming passion for Christ. In the words of the hymn, may the things of earth grow dim, in the light of his glory and grace.

JOURNALING

How would you explain to a highly moral friend that a person does not make it to heaven on the basis of living a "good" life?

FOR FURTHER READING

To complete the book of Philippians during this twelve-part study, read Philippians 3:1–11. For more Bible passages on the grace and glory of Christ, read Isaiah 53:4–6; Luke 15:11–31; John 4:1–42; Romans 3:20–28; Galatians 3:1–14; Ephesians 2:8–9; and Colossians 1:13–23.

ETERNAL FOCUS

One thing I do: Forgetting what is behind and straining toward what is ahead, I press on toward the goal to win the prize for which God has called me heavenward in Christ Jesus.

Philippians 3:13–14

REFLECTION

There are some who argue it's possible to be so "heavenly minded" that one is no earthly good. There are others, such as author C.S. Lewis, who insist those who think the most about the next world to come end up doing the most in this world. Which view do you think is right? What are your own habits and attitudes regarding heaven?

SITUATION

When the apostle Paul met Jesus on the road to Damascus, it forever revolutionized his life. Up to that point he had been a strict follower of the Jewish law and zealous to honor all the Jewish customs, but his encounter with Christ completely transformed his understanding of salvation and infused him with new purpose (see Acts 22:3–21). Paul's driving passion was now, as he relates in this next section of his letter, to press on toward the goal to which God has called him: *to know Christ and make him known to the world.* Paul recognized that his time on this earth was short, and he had to use the moments God had given him to prepare for eternity.

OBSERVATION

*Read Philippians 3:12–21 from the New International
Version or the New King James Version.*

New International Version

[12] Not that I have already obtained all this, or have already arrived at my goal, but I press on to take hold of that for which Christ Jesus took hold of me. [13] Brothers and sisters, I do not consider myself yet to have taken hold of it. But one thing I do: Forgetting what is behind and straining toward what is ahead, [14] I press on toward the goal to win the prize for which God has called me heavenward in Christ Jesus.

[15] All of us, then, who are mature should take such a view of things. And if on some point you think differently, that too God will make clear to you. [16] Only let us live up to what we have already attained.

[17] Join together in following my example, brothers and sisters, and just as you have us as a model, keep your eyes on those who live as we do. [18] For, as I have often told you before and now tell you again even with tears, many live as enemies of the cross of Christ. [19] Their destiny is destruction, their god is their stomach, and their glory is in their shame. Their mind is set on earthly things. [20] But our citizenship is in heaven. And we eagerly await a Savior from there, the Lord Jesus Christ, [21] who, by the power that enables him to bring everything under his control, will transform our lowly bodies so that they will be like his glorious body.

New King James Version

[12] Not that I have already attained, or am already perfected; but I press on, that I may lay hold of that for which Christ Jesus has also laid hold of me. [13] Brethren, I do not count myself to have apprehended; but one thing I do, forgetting those things which are behind and reaching forward to those things which are ahead, [14] I press toward the goal for the prize of the upward call of God in Christ Jesus.

¹⁵ Therefore let us, as many as are mature, have this mind; and if in anything you think otherwise, God will reveal even this to you. ¹⁶ Nevertheless, to the degree that we have already attained, let us walk by the same rule, let us be of the same mind.

¹⁷ Brethren, join in following my example, and note those who so walk, as you have us for a pattern. ¹⁸ For many walk, of whom I have told you often, and now tell you even weeping, that they are the enemies of the cross of Christ: ¹⁹ whose end is destruction, whose god is their belly, and whose glory is in their shame—who set their mind on earthly things. ²⁰ For our citizenship is in heaven, from which we also eagerly wait for the Savior, the Lord Jesus Christ, ²¹ who will transform our lowly body that it may be conformed to His glorious body, according to the working by which He is able even to subdue all things to Himself.

EXPLORATION

1. How does Paul describe his own spiritual journey with Christ? What is his primary aim?

_____

_____

_____

_____

2. What does this say about the need for perseverance in following Jesus?

_____

_____

_____

3. What does Paul teach here about goals, motivation, and living an intentional life?

_____

_____

_____

4. Why are spiritual mentors and spiritual disciplines so important?

_____

_____

_____

5. What does it mean to live as an "enemy" of Christ?

_____

_____

_____

6. It grieved Paul to see people living and dying without Christ. On the other hand, thoughts of the world to come gave him great joy. How would you describe these two different ideas?

_____

_____

_____

INSPIRATION

When I was a young man, I had plenty of people to wipe away my tears. I had two big sisters who put me under their wings. I had a dozen or so aunts and uncles. I had a mother who worked nights as a nurse and days as a mother—exercising both professions with tenderness. I even had a brother three years my elder who felt sorry for me occasionally.

But when I think about someone wiping away my tears, I think about Dad. His hands were callused and tough, his fingers short and stubby. And when my father wiped away a tear, he seemed to wipe it away forever. There was something in his touch that took away more than the drop of hurt from my cheek. It also took away my fear.

John says that someday God will wipe away your tears. The same hands that stretched the heavens will touch your cheeks. The same hands that formed the mountains will caress your face. The same hands that curled in agony as the Roman spike cut through will someday cup your face and brush away your tears. Forever.

When you think of a world where there will be no reason to cry, ever, doesn't it make you want to go home?

John declares, "There will be no more death . . ." (Revelation 21:4). Can you imagine it? A world with no hearses or morgues or cemeteries or tombstones? Can you imagine a world with no spades of dirt thrown on caskets? No names chiseled into marble? No funerals? No black dresses? No black wreaths?

If one of the joys of the ministry is a bride descending the church aisle, one of the griefs is a body encased in a shiny box in front of the pulpit. It's never easy to say goodbye. It's never easy to walk away. The hardest task in this world is to place a final kiss on cold lips that cannot kiss in return. The hardest thing in this world is to say goodbye.

In the next world, John says, "goodbye" will never be spoken. (From *The Applause of Heaven* by Max Lucado.)

REACTION

7. Paul and the other apostles spoke and wrote frequently about heaven. What are some practical ways an eternal perspective can make a huge difference in your everyday life?

_____

_____

_____

_____

_____

8. How can Christians avoid a sense of complacency in the spiritual life?

_____

_____

_____

9. Why does Paul use the metaphor of a race to describe the Christian life? What does he mean by alluding to "the prize" (verse 14)?

_____

_____

_____

10. Who are some older and wiser Christians you look to as examples? In what ways do you try to pattern your life after theirs?

_____

_____

_____

11. What would you do differently if you decided to live each day gripped by the reality that you are a citizen of heaven?

_____

_____

_____

12. Paul mentions _eagerly_ awaiting the return of Christ. Do you get excited by the thought of eternity with God? Why or why not?

_____

_____

_____

LIFE LESSONS

There are so many ways to say it: "This earth is not our home." "We are only passing through." "I am bound for the Promised Land." Given the fragility and brevity of this life and the certainty of the world to come, how should we live today? We need spiritual leaders and mentors who will exhort us to resist the fleeting attractions of this dying world. We need fellow pilgrims to journey with us along the path. Do you have such people in your life? Are you a vital part of a healthy Christian community? Ask God for strong Christian influences who can keep pointing you to the things that are true.

DEVOTION

Lord, thank you for the hope of heaven. Thank you for the promise that one day you will make everything right and all things new. Help us to become more and more convinced of this truth, with the result that we live with ever-increasing passion and power.

JOURNALING

What are your biggest questions about eternity?

_____

_____

_____

_____

_____

_____

_____

_____

_____

FOR FURTHER READING

To complete the book of Philippians during this twelve-part study, read Philippians 3:12–21. For more Bible passages about living with an eternal perspective, read Matthew 6:19–21; John 14:1–8; 2 Corinthians 4:16–18; Colossians 3:1–4; Hebrews 11:24–28; 12:1–3; and 1 Peter 1:3–5.

THE PEACE OF GOD

*Be anxious for nothing, but in everything by prayer
and supplication, with thanksgiving, let your
requests be made known to God; and the peace of
God, which surpasses all understanding, will guard
your hearts and minds through Christ Jesus.*

PHILIPPIANS 4:6–7 NKJV

REFLECTION

We have financial, medical, educational, and spiritual advantages that previous generations never imagined—and yet we have more counselors and psychiatrists seeing more patients and writing more prescriptions than at any other time in history. Why do you think so many people—and so many Christians—lack real peace of mind?

SITUATION

As Paul draws his letter of Philippians to a close, he will once again call on the believers to "stand firm" and "be of the same mind in the Lord" (Philippians 1:27; 4:1–2). But this time, Paul will leave them with some practical instructions for how they can, in fact, live in such a way: by rejoicing in the Lord always, showing gentleness to all, refusing to give in to anxieties, and by presenting their needs—with *thanksgiving*—to the heavenly Father. As Paul notes, following this "prescription" for life leads to a wonderful result: the perfect peace of God.

OBSERVATION

*Read Philippians 4:1–7 from the New International
Version or the New King James Version.*

NEW INTERNATIONAL VERSION

¹ Therefore, my brothers and sisters, you whom I love and long for, my joy and crown, stand firm in the Lord in this way, dear friends!

² I plead with Euodia and I plead with Syntyche to be of the same mind in the Lord. ³ Yes, and I ask you, my true companion, help these women since they have contended at my side in the cause of the gospel, along with Clement and the rest of my co-workers, whose names are in the book of life.

⁴ Rejoice in the Lord always. I will say it again: Rejoice! ⁵ Let your gentleness be evident to all. The Lord is near. ⁶ Do not be anxious about anything, but in every situation, by prayer and petition, with thanksgiving, present your requests to God. ⁷ And the peace of God, which transcends all understanding, will guard your hearts and your minds in Christ Jesus.

NEW KING JAMES VERSION

¹ Therefore, my beloved and longed-for brethren, my joy and crown, so stand fast in the Lord, beloved.

² I implore Euodia and I implore Syntyche to be of the same mind in the Lord. ³ And I urge you also, true companion, help these women who labored with me in the gospel, with Clement also, and the rest of my fellow workers, whose names are in the Book of Life.

⁴ Rejoice in the Lord always. Again I will say, rejoice!

⁵ Let your gentleness be known to all men. The Lord is at hand.

⁶ Be anxious for nothing, but in everything by prayer and supplication, with thanksgiving, let your requests be made known to God; ⁷ and the peace of God, which surpasses all understanding, will guard your hearts and minds through Christ Jesus.

EXPLORATION

1. Two women in the church at Philippi, Euodia and Syntyche, were obviously involved in some kind of conflict. Why are disagreements so stressful and draining to a church?

2. Paul urges an unnamed person in Philippians 4:3 to help mediate the dispute between these two women. How skilled are you at helping resolve conflicts?

3. How can a spirit of rejoicing help combat stressful and anxious situations?

4. What role does allowing "your gentleness be evident to all" (verse 5) play in creating unity and reducing stress in a community?

5. How does a belief in the imminent return of the Lord help bring you peace?

6. How does prayer play a part in bringing God's peace? Why is it important to come to God not just with requests but with thankfulness?

INSPIRATION

When mariners describe a tempest that no sailor can escape, they call it a perfect storm. Not perfect in the sense of ideal, but perfect in the sense of combining factors. All the elements, such as hurricane-force winds plus a cold front plus a downpour of rain, work together to create the insurmountable disaster. The winds alone would be a challenge; but the winds plus the cold plus the rain? The perfect recipe for disaster.

You needn't be a fisherman to experience a perfect storm. All you need is a layoff *plus* a recession. A disease *plus* a job transfer. A relationship breakup *plus* a college rejection. We can handle one challenge . . . but two or three at a time? One wave after another, gale forces followed by thunderstorms? It's enough to make you wonder, *Will I survive?*

Paul's answer to that question is profound and concise. "The peace of God, which surpasses all understanding, will guard your hearts and minds through Christ Jesus" (Philippians 4:7).

As we do our part (rejoice in the Lord, pursue a gentle spirit, pray about everything, and cling to gratitude), God does his part. He bestows upon us the peace of God. Note, this is not a peace from God. Our Father gives us the very peace of God. He downloads the tranquility of the throne room into our world, resulting in an inexplicable calm. We should be worried, but we aren't. We should be upset, but we are comforted. The peace of God transcends all logic, scheming, and efforts to explain it.

This kind of peace is not a human achievement. It is a gift from above. "Peace I leave with you; my peace I give you. I do not give to you as

the world gives. Do not let your hearts be troubled and do not be afraid"
(John 14:27).

Jesus promises you his vintage of peace! The peace that calmed his
heart when he was falsely accused. The peace that steadied his voice
when he spoke to Pilate. The peace that kept his thoughts clear and heart
pure as he hung on the cross. This was his peace. This can be your peace.
(From *Anxious for Nothing* by Max Lucado.)

REACTION

7. What are some "perfect storms" that you have weathered? How did
you get through these difficult times?

_____

_____

_____

8. What part do Christians play in reducing anxiety? What part does
God play?

_____

_____

_____

9. What stresses you more—being in a conflict or having to referee a
conflict between other people? Why?

_____

_____

_____

10. How would you define what Paul means by "the peace of God"
(verse 7)?

_____

_____

_____

11. How is the peace of God different from other kinds of peace?

_____

_____

_____

12. Of all the topics Paul mentions here (resolving conflicts with others, rejoicing, showing gentleness, remembering the return of the Lord, praying about situations), which would bring the most peace to your life?

_____

_____

_____

LIFE LESSONS

Can you think of anything the world needs more than peace? Look around your neighborhood at all the squabbling spouses and fractured friendships. Listen to people at work talk about their restless and stressful lives. Watch the news and see the tragic victims of crime and war. Hear the litany of scary reports of disease and doom. As Christians, we have the opportunity (and the responsibility) to show the world a different and better way. How? By living in peace with our fellow Christians. By trusting God to pour out his incomprehensible peace in life's anxious times. And by never forgetting the words of Jesus, "Blessed are the peacemakers, for they will be called children of God" (Matthew 5:9).

DEVOTION

Lord, fill us with a desire for unity. Fill us with joy. Fill us with gentleness and kindness and the firm conviction that your return is soon. Fill us with a thankful spirit and a consuming desire to seek you. Help us to realize that when we are filled with these things, there will be no room in our hearts for worry.

JOURNALING

What items can you list (relationships, situations, trials) that are currently causing you stress? What can you realistically do about each item you listed?

_____

_____

_____

_____

_____

_____

_____

_____

_____

_____

_____

_____

_____

_____

_____

_____

_____

FOR FURTHER READING

To complete the book of Philippians during this twelve-part study, read Philippians 4:1–7. For more Bible passages on experiencing God's peace, read Psalm 4:6–8; Isaiah 26:3–5; Luke 12:22–26; John 14:25–27; 16:31–33; Romans 12:16–18; 1 Thessalonians 5:12–15; and Hebrews 12:11–14.

IT'S ALL IN YOUR MIND

Whatever is true, whatever is noble, whatever is right, whatever is pure, whatever is lovely, whatever is admirable—if anything is excellent or praiseworthy—think about such things
PHILIPPIANS 4:8

REFLECTION

Don't we all need a makeover? Worrywarts need peace. Those who struggle with envy need to learn to be content. Truth be told, most of us *hunger* to be different. So, here is one of the most valuable questions you can ponder . . . how exactly *do* people change?

SITUATION

The apostle Paul has provided some guidelines for how the believers can adopt the example of Christ and live at peace with one another. In this next section, he adds one additional method that Christians can employ to fight against fear and anxiety: dwelling on thoughts that are God-honoring. Paul knows the battle against the enemy begins in the mind, and by adopting thoughts are true, noble, pure, and right, we have the proper mindset to wage the fight.

OBSERVATION

Read Philippians 4:8–13 from the New International Version or the New King James Version.

New International Version

8 Finally, brothers and sisters, whatever is true, whatever is noble, whatever is right, whatever is pure, whatever is lovely, whatever is admirable—if anything is excellent or praiseworthy—think about such things. 9 Whatever you have learned or received or heard from me, or seen in me—put it into practice. And the God of peace will be with you.

10 I rejoiced greatly in the Lord that at last you renewed your concern for me. Indeed, you were concerned, but you had no opportunity to show it. 11 I am not saying this because I am in need, for I have learned to be content whatever the circumstances. 12 I know what it is to be in need, and I know what it is to have plenty. I have learned the secret of being content in any and every situation, whether well fed or hungry, whether living in plenty or in want. 13 I can do all this through him who gives me strength.

New King James Version

8 Finally, brethren, whatever things are true, whatever things are noble, whatever things are just, whatever things are pure, whatever things are lovely, whatever things are of good report, if there is any virtue and if there is anything praiseworthy—meditate on these things. 9 The things which you learned and received and heard and saw in me, these do, and the God of peace will be with you.

10 But I rejoiced in the Lord greatly that now at last your care for me has flourished again; though you surely did care, but you lacked opportunity. 11 Not that I speak in regard to need, for I have learned in whatever state I am, to be content: 12 I know how to be abased, and I know how to abound. Everywhere and in all things I have learned both to be full and to be hungry, both to abound and to suffer need. 13 I can do all things through Christ who strengthens me.

EXPLORATION

1. Why do you think your thoughts are so important when it comes to following Christ?

_____

_____

_____

_____

2. What is significant about the qualities Paul chose for evaluating and ordering your thoughts?

_____

_____

_____

_____

_____

3. What conclusions, if any, should you draw from the fact Paul speaks about _thinking_ in verse 8 and about _doing_ in verse 9?

_____

_____

_____

_____

_____

4. Paul seems to be suggesting that when your thinking is spiritually sound, your circumstances will stop stealing your joy. How have you experienced this in your life?

_____

_____

_____

5. Remember that Paul was in prison when he penned this letter to the Philippians. Given this, how can he state that he is "not saying this because I am in need" (verse 11)?

_____

_____

_____

_____

_____

6. What thought strengthened Paul and enabled him to be content during even this hard circumstance and his other times of want?

_____

_____

_____

_____

INSPIRATION

You and I are infected by destructive thoughts. Computer viruses have names like Klez, Anna Kournikova, and ILOVEYOU. Mental viruses are known as anxiety, bitterness, anger, guilt, shame, greed, and insecurity. They worm their way into your system and diminish, even disable, your mind. We call these DTPs: _destructive thought patterns._

Actually, I'm the only one to call them DTPs. But do you have them?

When you see the successful, are you jealous? When you see the struggler, are you pompous? If someone gets on your bad side, is that person as likely to get on your good side as I am to win the Tour-de-France?

Ever argue with someone in your mind? Rehash or rehearse your hurts? Do you assume the worst about the future? If so, you suffer from DTPs.

What would your world be like without them? Had no dark or destructive thought ever entered your mind, how would you be different? Suppose you could live your life sans any guilt, lust, vengeance, insecurity, or fear. Never wasting mental energy on gossip or scheming. Would you be different? . . .

Oh, to be DTP-free. No energy lost, no time wasted. Wouldn't such a person be energetic and wise? A lifetime of healthy and holy thoughts would render anyone a joyful genius. . . .

A lot like the twelve-year-old boy seated in the temple of Jerusalem. Though he was beardless and unadorned, this boy's thoughts were profound. . . . When it comes to his purity of mind, we are given this astounding claim: Christ "knew no sin" (2 Corinthians 5:21 NKJV). Peter says Jesus "committed no sin, and no deceit was found in his mouth" (1 Peter 2:22). John lived next to him for three years and concluded, "In Him there is no sin" (1 John 3:5 NKJV) . . .

But does this matter? Does the perfection of Christ affect us? If he were a distant Creator, the answer would be no. But since he is a next door Savior, the reply is a supersized yes!

Remember the twelve-year-old boy in the temple? The one with sterling thoughts and a Teflon mind? Guess what. That is God's goal for you! You are made to be like Christ! God's priority is that you be "transformed by the renewing of your mind" (Romans 12:2). You may have been born virus-prone, but you don't have to live that way . . . God can change your mind. (From *Next Door Savior* by Max Lucado.)

REACTION

7. What are some of your most destructive thought patterns?

_____

_____

_____

_____

8. How disciplined is your mind? Do you work at corralling untrue and unhealthy thoughts?

9. What process do you employ for dwelling on just those thoughts that are true, noble, right, pure, lovely, and admirable?

10. How confident would you be in telling a younger Christian what Paul told the Philippians in verse 9? Why?

11. Would you describe yourself as a contented person? Why or why not?

12. In what ways are you continually depending on Jesus for your strength?

_____

_____

_____

_____

_____

_____

LIFE LESSONS

Mention *meditation* and most Christians either glaze over or tense up. Perhaps you, too, view this practice as incomprehensible or even incompatible with your faith. But in fact meditation, is both described and prescribed in Scripture (see Joshua 1:8 and Psalm 119:27). At the most basic level, meditation is simply focusing our minds on a thought or set of thoughts. It is chewing on an idea like a cow might chew its cud. It is letting our minds marinate in (soak up) a certain idea. We all do this. Even worrying is a (negative) form of meditating—it is dwelling on possible bad outcomes. Paul is telling us here that the path to a joy-filled life of contentment and peace is by learning to meditate on what God says is true. Will you do this today?

DEVOTION

Father, we have so much to learn. We realize our minds are often focused on things that are untrue, unworthy, unlovely, and unhealthy. By your Spirit, teach us how to reprogram our thoughts so they line up with yours. Impress upon us the great truth that our lives will never change until our minds are changed.

JOURNALING

Think about a recent incident in which you got emotional. What thoughts contributed to your strong feelings? How do those thoughts compare with what God says is true?

FOR FURTHER READING

To complete the book of Philippians during this twelve-part study, read Philippians 4:8–13. For more Bible passages on renewing your mind, read Joshua 1:8–9; Psalm 119:13–16, 46–48, 77–80, 97–99; Romans 12:1–2; 2 Corinthians 10:3–6; Ephesians 4:20–24; and Colossians 3:9–10.

GENEROSITY

*And my God shall supply all
your need according to His
riches in glory by Christ Jesus.*
PHILIPPIANS 4:19 NKJV

REFLECTION

At birthdays, weddings, anniversaries, births, graduations, and holidays, we give and receive presents. It's hard to imagine a world without this practice. Would you say that you more comfortable giving or receiving gifts? Why?

SITUATION

Paul began his letter to the Philippians by expressing his thanks for the way in which they had partnered with him in sharing the gospel. He concludes in much the same manner: by expressing his gratitude for the financial gift they have sent to him. In doing so, Paul follows the typical writing conventions of his day, making sure the believers know he has "learned to be content whatever the circumstances" (Philippians 4:11), so his words will not be taken as a request to receive more funds from them. Paul's closing words remind us of many important biblical truths, including the need to be generous with the resources God has given to us.

OBSERVATION

*Read Philippians 4:14–23 from the New International
Version or the New King James Version.*

NEW INTERNATIONAL VERSION

[14] Yet it was good of you to share in my troubles. [15] Moreover, as you Philippians know, in the early days of your acquaintance with the gospel, when I set out from Macedonia, not one church shared with me in the matter of giving and receiving, except you only; [16] for even when I was in Thessalonica, you sent me aid more than once when I was in need. [17] Not that I desire your gifts; what I desire is that more be credited to your account. [18] I have received full payment and have more than enough. I am amply supplied, now that I have received from Epaphroditus the gifts you sent. They are a fragrant offering, an acceptable sacrifice, pleasing to God. [19] And my God will meet all your needs according to the riches of his glory in Christ Jesus.

[20] To our God and Father be glory for ever and ever. Amen.

[21] Greet all God's people in Christ Jesus. The brothers and sisters who are with me send greetings. [22] All God's people here send you greetings, especially those who belong to Caesar's household.

[23] The grace of the Lord Jesus Christ be with your spirit. Amen.

NEW KING JAMES VERSION

[14] Nevertheless you have done well that you shared in my distress. [15] Now you Philippians know also that in the beginning of the gospel, when I departed from Macedonia, no church shared with me concerning giving and receiving but you only. [16] For even in Thessalonica you sent aid once and again for my necessities. [17] Not that I seek the gift, but I seek the fruit that abounds to your account. [18] Indeed I have all and abound. I am full, having received from Epaphroditus the things sent from you, a sweet-smelling aroma, an acceptable sacrifice, well pleasing to God. [19] And my God shall supply all your need according to His riches in

glory by Christ Jesus. ²⁰ Now to our God and Father be glory forever and ever. Amen.

²¹ Greet every saint in Christ Jesus. The brethren who are with me greet you. ²² All the saints greet you, but especially those who are of Caesar's household.

²³ The grace of our Lord Jesus Christ be with you all. Amen.

EXPLORATION

1. What are some ways believers can actively share in the troubles of others?

2. According to this passage, what were the Philippians' giving habits?

3. What do you think Paul means when he says that he does not desire the believers' gifts, but that "more be credited to your account" (verse 17)?

4. Paul writes of the good that comes from giving. What good comes to the giver?

5. What determines whether a gift gets praised (as in this case) or is scorned by God (see, for example, Proverbs 15:8; Isaiah 1:10–17; and Malachi 1:8)?

_____

_____

_____

_____

6. What is the promise to those who give with the right attitude?

_____

_____

_____

INSPIRATION

Today I will make a difference. I will begin by controlling my thoughts. A person is the product of his thoughts. I want to be happy and hopeful. Therefore, I will have thoughts that are happy and hopeful. I refuse to be victimized by my circumstances. I will not let petty inconveniences such as stoplights, long lines, and traffic jams be my masters. I will avoid negativism and gossip. Optimism will be my companion, and victory will be my hallmark.

Today I will make a difference. I will be grateful for the twenty-four hours that are before me. Time is a precious commodity. I refuse to allow what little time I have to be contaminated by self-pity, anxiety, or boredom. I will face this day with the joy of a child and the courage of a giant. I will drink each minute as though it is my last. When tomorrow comes, today will be gone forever. While it is here, I will use it for loving and giving.

Today I will make a difference. I will not let past failures haunt me. Even though my life is scarred with mistakes, I refuse to rummage through my trash heap of failures. I will admit them. I will correct them. I will press on. Victoriously. No failure is fatal. It's okay to stumble; I will get up. It's okay to fail; I will rise again.

Today I will make a difference. I will spend time with those I love. My spouse, my children, my family. A man can own the world but be poor for the lack of love. A man can own nothing and yet be wealthy in relationships. Today I will spend at least five minutes with the significant people in my world. Five *quality* minutes of talking or hugging or thanking or listening. Five undiluted minutes with my mate, children, and friends.

Today I will make a difference. (From *Shaped by God* by Max Lucado.)

REACTION

7. In what ways can even your small gifts and offerings make a difference in others' lives?

_____

_____

_____

_____

_____

8. In supporting Paul, the Philippians were literally supporting a missionary. What are the implications of this for you and your church?

_____

_____

_____

_____

_____

9. Many people feel churches overly emphasize giving. Do you feel this a fair assessment? Why or why not?

_____

_____

_____

_____

_____

10. God says, "Every animal of the forest is mine, and the cattle on a thousand hills" (Psalm 50:10). He doesn't need our money. So why does the Bible say so much about giving?

11. What are your giving habits? Do you give regularly and generously? Why or why not?

12. How would you describe the difference between *tithing*—the practice of giving ten percent of your income to God—and giving *offerings* to your church?

LIFE LESSONS

The Bible is clear: money is a blessing, a danger, a stewardship, a test, and a tool. What we do with material wealth is a reliable indicator of our spiritual health. How we behave with money reveals what we truly believe. If we are tight-fisted, hoard, and think constantly of getting but only rarely of giving, we disclose that we do not really trust in God's goodness or have faith that his supplies are infinite. At issue in this area of giving is not the amount but our attitude. Do we see giving as a duty or a delight? Do we give grudgingly or with joy? Hear again the challenge of Jesus—to use your worldly wealth for his eternal purposes (see Luke 16:1–13).

DEVOTION

Lord, teach us the paradoxical truth that the way we "get a grip" on this subject of giving is by "loosening our grip" on our money. Remind us again and again of how generous you have been with us so that we might more willingly and gladly pass on your blessings to others.

JOURNALING

Imagine spreading out your financial records in front of God. What do you think he might say about the way you use the resources he has entrusted to you?

_____

_____

_____

_____

_____

_____

_____

_____

_____

_____

FOR FURTHER READING

To complete the book of Philippians during this twelve-part study, read Philippians 4:14–23. For more Bible passages on tithing and giving, read Deuteronomy 14:22–29; 1 Chronicles 29:1–9; Proverbs 3:9–10; Malachi 3:8–10; Matthew 10:7–15; Acts 11:27–30; and 2 Corinthians 9:6–8.

LEADER'S GUIDE FOR SMALL GROUPS

Thank you for your willingness to lead a group through *Life Lessons from Philippians*. The rewards of being a leader are different from those of participating, and we hope you find your own walk with Jesus deepened by this experience. During the twelve lessons in this study, you will guide your group through selected passages in Philippians and explore the key themes of the letter. There are several elements in this leader's guide that will help you as you structure your study and reflection time, so be sure to follow along and take advantage of each one.

BEFORE YOU BEGIN

Before your first meeting, make sure the group members have their own copy of the *Life Lessons from Philippians* study guide so they can follow along and have their answers written out ahead of time. Alternately, you can hand out the guides at your first meeting and give the group some time to look over the material and ask any preliminary questions. Be sure to send a sheet around the room during that first meeting and have the members write down their name, phone number, and email address so you can keep in touch with them during the week.

There are two ways to structure the duration of the study. You can choose to cover each lesson individually for a total of twelve weeks of discussion, or you can combine two lessons together per week for a total of six weeks of discussion. (Note that if the group members read the selected passages of Scripture for each lesson, they will cover the entire book of Philippians during the study.) The following table illustrates these options:

Twelve-Week Format

Week	Lessons Covered	Reading
1	Praying for Others	Philippians 1:1–11
2	Triumph in Trouble	Philippians 1:12–18
3	Standing Firm	Philippians 1:19–30
4	All for One	Philippians 2:1–4
5	Ultimate Servanthood	Philippians 2:5–11
6	Shining for Christ	Philippians 2:12–18
7	Role Models	Philippians 2:19–30
8	Right Standing with God	Philippians 3:1–11
9	Eternal Focus	Philippians 3:12–21
10	The Peace of God	Philippians 4:1–7
11	It's All in Your Mind	Philippians 4:8–13
12	Generosity	Philippians 4:14–23

Six-Week Format

Week	Lessons Covered	Reading
1	Praying for Others / Triumph in Trouble	Philippians 1:1–18
2	Standing Firm / All for One	Philippians 1:19–2:4
3	Ultimate Servanthood / Shining for Christ	Philippians 2:5–18
4	Role Models / Right Standing with God	Philippians 2:19–3:11
5	Eternal Focus / The Peace of God	Philippians 3:12–4:7
6	It's All in Your Mind / Generosity	Philippians 4:8–23

Generally, the ideal size you will want for the group is between eight to ten people, which ensures everyone will have enough time to participate in discussions. If you have more people, you might want to break up the main group into smaller subgroups. Encourage those who show up at the first meeting to commit to attending the duration of the study, as this will help the group members get to know each other, create stability for the group, and help you know how to prepare each week.

Each of the lessons begins with a brief reflection that highlights the theme you will be discussing that week. As you begin your group time, have the group members briefly respond to the opening question to get them thinking about the topic at hand. Some people may want to tell a long story in response to one of these questions, but the goal is to keep the answers brief. Ideally, you want everyone in the group to get a chance to answer, so try to keep the responses to just a few minutes. If you have more talkative group members, say up front that everyone needs to limit his or her answer to two minutes.

Give the group members a chance to answer, but tell them to feel free to pass if they wish. With the rest of the study, it's generally not a good idea to have everyone answer every question—a free-flowing discussion is more desirable. But with the opening reflection question, you can go around the circle. Encourage shy people to share, but don't force them.

Before your first meeting, let the group members know how the lessons are broken down. During your group discussion time the members will be drawing on the answers they wrote to the Exploration and Reaction sections, so encourage them to always complete these ahead of time. Also, invite them to bring any questions and insights they uncovered while reading to your next meeting, especially if they had a breakthrough moment or if they didn't understand something they read.

WEEKLY PREPARATION

As the leader, there are a few things you should do to prepare for each meeting:

- *Read through the lesson.* This will help you to become familiar with the content and know how to structure the discussion times.
- *Decide which questions you want to discuss.* Depending on how you structure your group time, you may not be able to cover every

question. So select the questions ahead of time that you absolutely want the group to explore.

- *Be familiar with the questions you want to discuss.* When the group meets you'll be watching the clock, so you want to make sure you are familiar with the Bible study questions you have selected. You can then spend time in the passage again when the group meets. In this way, you'll ensure you have the passage more deeply in your mind than your group members.

- *Pray for your group.* Pray for your group members throughout the week and ask God to lead them as they study his Word.

- *Bring extra supplies to your meeting.* The members should bring their own pens for writing notes, but it's a good idea to have extras available for those who forget. You may also want to bring paper and additional Bibles.

Note that in many cases there will not be one "right" answer to the question. Answers will vary, especially when the group members are being asked to share their personal experiences.

STRUCTURING THE DISCUSSION TIME

You will need to determine with your group how long you want to meet each week so you can plan your time accordingly. Generally, most groups like to meet for either sixty minutes or ninety minutes, so you could use one of the following schedules:

Section	60 Minutes	90 Minutes
WELCOME (members arrive and get settled)	5 minutes	10 minutes
REFLECTION (discuss the opening question for the lesson)	10 minutes	15 minutes
DISCUSSION (discuss the Bible study questions in the Exploration and Reaction sections)	35 minutes	50 minutes
PRAYER/CLOSING (pray together as a group and dismiss)	10 minutes	15 minutes

As the group leader, it is up to you to keep track of the time and keep things moving along according to your schedule. You might want to set a timer for each segment so both you and the group members know when your time is up. (Note that there are some good phone apps for timers that play a gentle chime or other pleasant sound instead of a disruptive noise.) Don't feel pressured to cover every question you have selected if the group has a good discussion going. Again, it's not necessary to go around the circle and make everyone share.

Don't be concerned if the group members are silent or slow to share. People are often quiet when they are pulling together their ideas, and this might be a new experience for them. Just ask a question and let it hang in the air until someone shares. You can then say, "Thank you. What about others? What came to you when you reflected on the passage?"

GROUP DYNAMICS

Leading a group through *Life Lessons from Philippians* will prove to be highly rewarding both to you and your group members—but that doesn't mean you will not encounter any challenges along the way! Discussions can get off track. Group members may not be sensitive to the needs and ideas of others. Some might worry they will be expected to talk about matters that make them feel awkward. Others may express comments that result in disagreements. To help ease this strain on you and the group, consider the following ground rules:

- When someone raises a question or comment that is off the main topic, suggest you deal with it another time, or, if you feel led to go in that direction, let the group know you will be spending some time discussing it.
- If someone asks a question you don't know how to answer, admit it and move on. At your discretion, feel free to invite group members to comment on questions that call for personal experience.

- If you find one or two people are dominating the discussion time, direct a few questions to others in the group. Outside the main group time, ask the more dominating members to help you draw out the quieter ones. Work to make them a part of the solution instead of the problem.
- When a disagreement occurs, encourage the group members to process the matter in love. Encourage those on opposite sides to restate what they heard the other side say about the matter, and then invite each side to evaluate if that perception is accurate. Lead the group in examining other Scriptures related to the topic and look for common ground.

When any of these issues arise, encourage your group members to follow the words from the Bible: "Love one another" (John 13:34), "If it is possible, as far as it depends on you, live at peace with everyone" (Romans 12:18), and, "Be quick to listen, slow to speak and slow to become angry" (James 1:19).

Thank you again for taking the time to lead your group. May God reward your efforts and dedication and make your time together in this study fruitful for his kingdom.

ALSO AVAILABLE IN THE
LIFE LESSONS SERIES

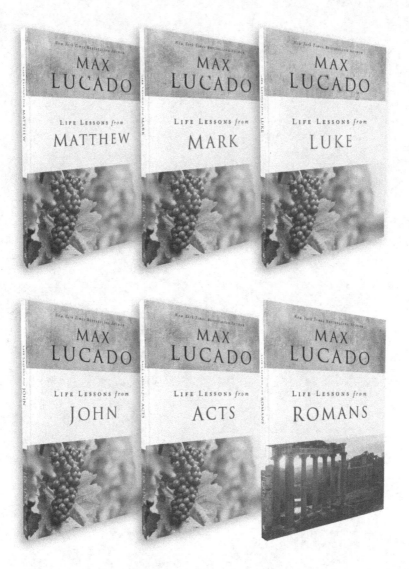

*Now available wherever books
and ebooks are sold.*